The Best Man's Handbook

From Ring to Reception

Andre Garrison

Detselig Enterprises Ltd.

Calgary, Alberta Canada

The Best Man's Handbook
© 1998 Andre Garrison

Canadian Cataloguing in Publication Data

Garrison, Andre, 1966-
The best man's handbook

Includes bibliographical references.
ISBN 1-55059-163-0

1. Wedding etiquette. 2. Masters of ceremonies. I. Title.
BJ2065.B45G37 1998   395.2'2   C98-910100-2

Detselig Enterprises Ltd.
210, 1220 Kensington Rd. N.W.
Calgary, Alberta T2N 3P5

Detselig Enterprises Ltd. appreciates the financial support for our 1998 publishing program, provided by Canadian Heritage and the Alberta Foundation for the Arts, a beneficiary of the Lottery Fund of the Government of Alberta.

Printed in Canada
ISBN 1-55059-163-0
SAN 115-0324

Cover Art by Dean Macdonald

I dedicate this book to all of those wonderful people who trusted me enough to let me be a part of their lives on that special day when they united as one.

I also dedicate this book to all those people who may benefit from these pages, and share in the experience of a wonderful beginning.

Congratulations and Good Luck

Table of Contents

Preface

When I originally considered writing this book, I stopped to ask myself why. I wondered if it was really necessary. I mean, I was certainly having my troubles, and so were many of my friends, but was that enough to actually sit down and write down what we had learned for others to read?

I had been to several weddings before I was finally asked by a very good friend of mine to be his best man. I was extremely elated at the prospect of standing up with my dear friend on what was to be the happiest day of his life. Then it suddenly dawned on me that I didn't have a clue what to do.

Oh sure, I had been to many weddings, and I had witnessed what went on. I fancy myself a pretty intelligent fellow, so how hard could it be, I thought? Well, I was in for a surprise.

Not wanting to be ill-prepared for such an important task, I did what any other sane man would do, and asked one of my friends who had already undertaken this privilege before me. I approached him in a matter-of-fact way and asked him to fill me in on the details of what he did and how he did it, that sort of thing.

Unfortunately, his response was anything but helpful. He had simply done what I was in the process of doing, asked somebody else who had done it before him. So, I asked somebody else and, to no large surprise, I got the same answer. Sure, there were more details to what went on other than merely doing what they were told to do, but I wasn't satisfied. I needed more answers, and it was becoming painfully obvious that I wasn't going to get them from any specific individual.

The library was my next stop – an obvious abundance of material would be jumping off the shelves at me. And to think that I asked my friends for advice first.

I looked for any or all books on the subject of being a best man, and was amazed to find that they didn't exist. There were several books on weddings, etc., so I gathered a sizeable collection and began reading.

Pages of text and hours of reading later brought me to the further conclusion that if I was going to act in a professional manner at my friend's wedding, I was to do it on my own. The little information that I had managed to collect was scattered at best, and certainly not enough for me to know anything further about being a best man. The trip to the library had proven futile.

It was because of this and for love of my friend that I decided to do whatever was necessary to make his wedding special, and several of my friends, having been in the same situation in the past or about to undertake a similar responsibility, agreed wholeheartedly.

Many of my friends and I became acquainted through playing on the same sports teams, and we would occasionally gather at each other's houses, or the pub afterwards, and discuss this matter. Those who had already been best men were deemed the professionals of the group, although ignorant as to their responsibilities as a whole. It seemed that the general consensus was that we were simply to fumble through it. Have a stag party, go to rehearsal, show up at the church, say thanks at the reception and that was it. It really seemed simple enough, but there was more.

As these nights continued several other stories were shared regarding friends of friends, or someone heard, or someone read somewhere . . . If that wasn't enough, we even started to tell stories about wedding mishaps; you know, things that go wrong at weddings. Well, that was the final straw. I would be ill-prepared but I wouldn't ruin my friend's wedding.

I started to work on the plan, and with the help of my friends, I put it into motion. Time was running out for me and I didn't have too much longer to prepare, the wedding being only a few weeks away.

I made a list of the general responsibilities and discussed with my friends all of the possible scenarios that might alter or add to these responsibilities. I wanted to be prepared for any contingency, just in case.

We then discussed all of the weddings that we had attended, and even solicited the help of a few parents in this regard. Many of these weddings followed the same guidelines, and were often simple, straightforward, boring affairs. However, the ones that really stuck out in our memories were ones where something had actually gone wrong, or where the couple did something entirely different from most weddings. In other words, they were fun, and since I wasn't going to ruin my friend's wedding for the sake of fun, I sought the other path, different.

On the day of the wedding, I reminded myself of all of the things I had learned in spite of my particular planning, and that no matter what should happen, I should relax and try to have fun because I was here for my friend.

I must say that it was one of the best weddings that I have ever been to, and many of my friends agreed. The wedding itself was not free of mishap, but not so overboard that it caused a lot of grief either. Naturally, it would have been so without our collective efforts, because in the end, all that is really important is that two people who love each other very much dedicate themselves to spending their lives together, and nothing that happens is going to change this fact. I realized this part way through the wedding when it dawned on me that I was being so nit-picky about detail, that I forgot my own advice.

Since that day, I have been to several other ceremonies and a best man at three of them. It seems that many of my friends were so impressed with my efforts that they wanted me to truly help them to make their wedding day more memorable.

I have learned a lot since becoming a best man, the most important being that no two wedding ceremonies are alike, and perhaps it is because of this that others in our group approach me, or send others to me for advice on what to do.

Thanks to their suggestive prodding, and the constant reminders, it has become easier to simply write a book about the subject and pass along a copy to those who need assistance.

After all, nobody is perfect, and although we often go through life doing things for ourselves, it's often nice every now and again to be offered help.

Introduction

So you've been asked to stand up with the groom at a wedding. The Best Man/Person is actually a misnomer, because you have to play second fiddle to the groom all day, but we really know that the title is true in its definition, the best. The first thing going through your mind is "arrrgh." I know how to go to a wedding (a guest). I even know how to get drunk and dance on the tables (an unwanted guest), now my friend wants me to stand up for him and emcee the wedding, and (hard swallow) make a speech. Oh, the agony, is a free meal really worth all of that? Sure, this will probably be one of those occasions in life where I get to increase the worth of my character, and look like a great guy in the eyes of my friend and his new bride, but can I really pull it off?

What happens at weddings these days? Will I have to give a speech or can I just stand next to the groom looking uncomfortable in my rented tuxedo? If you are already married, this chore may not be as difficult as you thought. Simply repeat everything that your best man did for you at your wedding. Of course, several factors do come to mind. First, was your wedding a disaster, partially due to your best man? If this is the case, you certainly don't want to have that entire incident repeated, unless of course you're one of those people who figure that if you didn't have any fun, why should anybody else? Second, chances are that someone in your circle of friends will be invited to this wedding. Friends tend to notice things like repeated speeches, especially at weddings. Finally, is it really that difficult to be a best man at a wedding these days?

Today's weddings present themselves in many different ways. Many people are straying from the traditional stiffness of the formal affair and trying to make the wedding something that it may not have been in the past, fun. Now I am not saying that people put on such splendid affairs that the guests felt as if it were a chore to attend rather than an honor. On the contrary, weddings of the past tended to be lavish affairs, elite social engagements where one could mingle with friends, family and possible business associates. But something was lacking in these grand presentations, something of great concern to all those attending – personality.

In the ornate affairs of the past, one was often invited to a wedding strictly because of social status, or family placement, making the ceremony a backdrop to social, business and personal concerns. For example, parents would often invite business associates and other high-status people, either to boost their own social standing in the community or to set the young couple up in society by introducing them to the powers that be. These circumstances still exist, and although they are not such widespread concerns, they do have their place for those who feel it's important.

Many of these weddings were presentations of two people exchanging their vows for a lifelong partnership, and the guests were merely witnesses to it all. The receptions were no different, a gathering for food and drink, often overshadowing the original purpose of the ceremony itself. This I feel made many of these affairs impersonal.

We've all been to weddings where we've felt that the bride and groom were unapproachable, that they were only decorations to admire from afar. Even as a guest at a wedding where two very close friends are united, people tend to veil themselves somewhat from the glow of the couple. Why do we do this? Are weddings such indifferent affairs that we can turn our heads away from the main reason for attending, just to enjoy our meals and the conversation at our immediate table?

Things have changed and many couples want their weddings to be a very personal affair, filled with laughter and gaiety. The wedding party wants to be the center of attention, but for different reasons. They don't want to be stared at in awe like circus freaks; they want to share their joy with all those in attendance. They want this moment to be special, not only for themselves and their families, but also for all of their friends and everybody else they thought important enough in their lives to share this moment with them.

As a best man at this wedding, you are one of these important people. Obviously, or you would not have been invited. But it goes a lot further than that. They care deeply for you and they really want you to be a part of things, not just an observer. You are not only to share in the wondrous joy that is their wedding; you are one of the reasons it is wondrous.

Being asked to be a best man

Asking someone to be a best man at a wedding is not an easy thing to do, especially because we are men. Men as a whole like to avoid such things, and often wait until the last minute to ask. This is where the happy bride-to-be steps in, and through constant reminders, the difficult question gets asked.

The fear of asking exists on a number of levels. Unlike the marriage proposal, where the fear of rejection figures prominently, asking your best friend to be your best man brings out fears that you may appear overly sentimental, especially if your relationship with your friend, close as you may be, is based on a manly lack of emotional expression. There still exists this silly fear of asking the closest friend in our lives to be just that, a close friend, and be a part of our wedding.

There are many ways one might be asked to become a best man, and it really depends on the personality of the individual asking, and the personality of the individual being asked. For the most part, people tend to have associations with people of the same temperament or of like personality, but I won't go into that because then this would be a book on psychology and not about men and weddings. Of course, such is not always the case. For example, a strong, outwardly-confident man might simply instruct his quiet friend that he is to be part of his wedding, whereas a mild, meek individual might have a lot of trouble approaching his more dominant friend to ask him to be his best man.

The bottom line is that it is an extremely important occasion and the question, however it comes, may have not been so easy to ask.

As men, a fact that few women know, we possess a special form of communication with each other. A sixth sense if you will. We can usually tell, for example, what the other is thinking when a beautiful woman walks into the room. Then there's those brief gestures that we share across a crowded room, trying to scope out location or favorites in the crowd, gestures that no one else may understand or even notice. Then there are team sports. Here we have the innate ability (some more than others) to be able to make a blind pass or shot to a friend, knowing without question that he is there.

It is for these reasons that when it comes to important questions in our lives, we often leave them unspoken. We assume that our friend will know exactly what's on our minds. After all, we are men. This, however, does not always work, blame it on bad connections if you will, and so we are forced to put our thoughts into words.

Many of us will simply blurt it out in a single breath.

"Hey, I'm getting married, want to be my best man?"

"Sure."

Others will take the scenic approach.

"Hey, did you see the game last night, wow, I can't believe they won."

"Yes, what a comeback."

"Oh, by the way, I asked Sandra to marry me, and she said yes. Want to be my best man?"

"Sure."

Then there is the more cordial or professional route.

"It is determined on this day, by myself and my bride-to-be, that on the sixth day of December, in the year of the Lord 1998, we shall be wed before the eyes of God, and a number of close friends and family. It is thereby sworn to ask you to be in attendance on this occasion to serve as my best man. That is, of course, if you would be sporting enough to patronize us on this day with your approval?"

"Jolly good of you to ask."

The sentimental path:

"Well, we've been friends for a very long time, and well, it just wouldn't be the same if you couldn't be there to be a part of our wedding. I think of you, not only as a friend, but as a brother, and that, well, I love you man. Would you be our best man?"

Sniff, sniff. "Sure."

Of course, your friend may not personally tell you this in words – men seldom do; however, I am quite certain that this is what has been left unsaid and articulated through some passive grunts and maybe even a handshake or a hug. Then we will immediately turn the conversation to sports.

The "I've known you for a long time" approach.

"Well?"

"Of course."

The "we've been friends forever" approach (like a couple of mimes without the make-up or silly costumes).

The groom-to-be approaches his friend, who gestures to him that there is a pretty girl across the street. The groom refuses to look. His friend, surprised, raises his eyebrows and shrugs his shoulders in a "really?" matter-of-fact way. The groom nods in assent, to which his friend smiles and extends his hand to congratulate his friend, patting him on the back. The groom then lowers his eyes, and stumbles in his motions, kicking a stone on the ground, as if he wants to ask his friend something difficult. His friend senses this and places his hand on his friend's shoulder. Their eyes meet and the groom offers the expression of "well," to which the friend happily nods. This done, they shake hands again and the friend tilts his head in the direction of the street and the two leave for a celebratory drink.

The ESP route:

"?"

"!"

If you stop and think for a moment how your friend initially asked you to be his best man, you may actually get an idea as to how difficult it was for him to ask. That being said, he is extremely glad that you said yes, and realizes that it wasn't so very difficult after all.

How to use this book

Now that you have been asked to perform this honorable duty, you realize that you have no idea what to do, and you didn't bother to factor in this variable when you so quickly answered your friend. So you went out and bought this book. Or your friend and his bride-to-be, knowing full well that you don't know what to do, got it for you. In either case, you are well on your way to truly becoming the best man.

To better acquaint yourself with how to use this book, I opted to start from the beginning, listing possible best man responsibilities and addressing them in chronological order (as best as I could). This way you should find yourself more adequately equipped for anything that you may face as the wedding day approaches, or as the wedding day itself progresses. So stop worrying, help is at hand, literally.

The chapters are broken down as follows:

Chapter 1: The Best Man's Responsibilities. This whole book contains the responsibilities of the best man, but I have detailed them specifically in this chapter so that you get a brief understanding of them without having to read the whole book if you don't feel like it. These responsibilities are, of course, illustrated in more detail in other chapters of the book for those who do feel like reading.

Chapter 2: The Bachelor Party. I wanted to start you off in the right direction, getting you inclined to fun and merriment before it actually sinks in that you might have to speak in front of a large group of people at the wedding. Several things are discussed here that I hope will help you to organize and stage one memorable stag/bachelor party. Keep in mind that I am not to be held responsible in any way, shape or form if things get out of hand, or if the wedding is called off because of certain things done by you and the groom-to-be.

Chapter 3: The Groom. If there wasn't a groom, there wouldn't be a best man, and if there wasn't a best man, you wouldn't be reading this book. In this chapter I strive to remind you why you were probably chosen to be the best man in the first place. Your friend or friends, as the case may be (including the bride), have a great deal of respect for you and they want you to be a part of their wedding. How you repay them can be a gesture that lasts a lifetime.

Chapter 4: The Bride. Like the groom, she is one of the more important people in the wedding party and she should thus be treated as such. But how do you fit into this? Well, the same way you would with the groom. He is probably your best friend and his happiness is very important to you. Thus, his bride-to-be, an immense source of his happiness, should be a concern of yours as well.

Chapter 5: Wedding Preparations. It wouldn't be a wedding without the wedding itself. Then of course it would just be a party with a bunch of well-dressed friends brought together to celebrate essentially nothing, not a lot unlike parties you had in college, except without the formal clothes. Here I point out how the best man can assist in the planning and preparations for the wedding. While the best man won't likely be held responsible for the event itself, I am hoping to give you a better understanding of the entire spectrum of what a wedding constitutes. That way, you'll truly know when something looks out of place or has gone seriously wrong. And, to better qualify what actually happens when something goes wrong, I have included several stories for reference.

Chapter 6: The Ring. The representation of love everlasting, and often a best man's downfall. This chapter is dedicated to avoiding the pitfalls of losing that small gold token.

Chapter 7: The Reception. For the most part it was an event to feed the people who attend the wedding bringing gifts, and has escalated into entertaining them as well. So be the entertainment, I'll show you how.

Chapter 8: The Emcee. As in Chapter 7, if you are the type of person who likes the spotlight, here is your big chance to impress your friends and their families. But, never the discerning emcee, you are just glad to have a microphone in your hand. If that's the case, this chapter is for you.

Chapter 9: Toasts and Speeches. You didn't really think that you could go to a wedding as a best man and not have to say at least something. Don't worry, it's not as bad as you think. A bit of humor and a few well-placed words and there won't be a dry eye in the house; again, great to impress the relatives, showing everybody that you have a sensitive side, and you haven't just been the bad influence in your friend's life all of these years.

For the more in-depth speech (hey, I said you might have to say something, and if you said one, what's one more?), there are several examples included here for your reference. Actually, your basic responsibility for words is usually restricted to toasting the bride and groom, but that role may have already been promised to someone of importance in the family. So you get pushed down the list, toasting the bridesmaids and/or finally, toasting the caterers. I'll show you how to get started using several examples which you can borrow and adjust for your own purposes.

Chapter 10: The Generic Speech. For those really devoid of any clue whatsoever on what to say, I've made it perfectly simple for you, including a generic speech so simple that all you have to do is to put the appropriate names in the right places and you're all set.

Chapter 11: Other Responsibilities. Hey, it's not my wedding, don't get mad at me. Some people like to benefit from as much help from their friends as possible. Don't blame me if your friends are that way and they want you to do everything. Luckily, now you can actually not worry about trying to back up your ignorance, and actually attempt to undertake some of these responsibilities, knowing how to carry them out.

This book offers a couple of things. The first is that it helps you, with the aid and experience of several others who have all gone through this before, to become a best man and undertake your responsibilities like a professional. Second, it illustrates that weddings are not always ceremoniously perfect, and that things can go wrong, so try to have fun and make the best of the wedding no matter what happens.

In the pages that follow, I hope that as the discerning best man you will want to use what you read and apply it for your own purposes. This book is meant merely as a guide and should not be (although it can be) followed to the letter. Every wedding is as different as the couples who get married, and this book demonstrates that fact several times over. Follow this book as a guide, an example of what needs to be done. Then apply this knowledge as it suits your needs and those of the wedding. Then let me know how it goes.

Chapter One
The Best Man's Responsibilities

What is a best man? There never seems to be a clear representation of what a best man is supposed to be responsible for at a wedding these days. Well, by definition:

> **BEST** (best) *adjective superlative of* GOOD **1.** Most excellent **2.** Most suitable, desirable, etc. **3.** Largest (the best part of the day)
> *adverb superlative of* WELL **1.** In the most excellent manner **2.** In the highest degree
> *noun* **1.** The most excellent person **2.** The utmost
> *verb* to defeat or outdo – **all for the best** ultimately good – **at best** under the most favorable conditions – **get the best of 1.** To defeat **2.** To outwit – **make the best of** to do as well as one can with

> **BEST MAN** the principal attendant of the bridegroom at a wedding

Knowing the definition doesn't exactly fill you with confidence, does it? The best man can play a multitude of roles in the ceremonies of this age, from the simplest forms of merely standing beside the groom to helping to organize the wedding itself. So how do you fit in, you ask? Well, the thing to do is very simple, ask the bride or the groom. They're easy to pick out. They're the ones running around, usually a bit tense, maybe stressed out and worried about making the most wonderful day of their lives perfect. I'll let you in on a little secret, they seldom are. Weddings are funny that way. In fact, I think something is supposed to go awry. It's like that old adage, something old, something new, something borrowed, something goes wrong . . . you see the trend here, don't you. (The problem is that they couldn't find a rhyme to go with wrong, so they just decided to take it out.)

Things do happen, and the best thing to do is to try and make light of the situation. If you can laugh at the small mishaps that plague weddings, they usually don't end up ruining the day, they end up making it more memorable.

So where does that leave you? Often it is the best man who is responsible for one or more of these wedding mishaps. Now I'm not telling you to deliberately sabotage your friend's wedding in the name of tradition, but I am saying that being ill-prepared, or basically ignorant of the situation, could be considered just cause. You can't just wing these affairs, going into it as if it will be a breeze. And if you screw up, you think to yourself "no biggy." Well, this may be the case for you, although I'm quite sure that the bride and groom have other notions.

It does pay to have a cool head and a good attitude. The bride and groom certainly have their hands full and the parents as well. Sometimes a refreshing indifference and relaxed disposition is exactly what the wedding needs, although each case dictates its own requirements.

This seems fairly straightforward enough. You are the principal attendant for the bridegroom at the wedding, and you are the best, ultimately good and most excellent. So now you know what you are, but you still don't understand what it is that you do other than to "attend."

Responsibilities defined

The responsibilities of a best man differ from wedding to wedding, so I will strive to include all possible scenarios. However, considering the absurdity of some peoples' tastes and needs, I'm quite sure that some items may have been overlooked. For instance, marriage rituals in remote parts of Africa require that the groom, in the company of his best friend, hunt and kill a wild animal, proving himself worthy of supplying food for his bride-to-be. The best man must also prove his worthiness to his best friend and his bride, in case illness or tragedy prevents the husband from adequately feeding his family. So the best man must also hunt and kill a wild animal. In some cases, the second to the best man must step in to fulfil these obligations, as the original best man is often hurt in the process.

Since this is not usually the prerequisite for most marriages, although it's not a bad idea, I will forego any details regarding hunting and gathering, greatly apologizing to those buying this book strictly on the basis of that information.

The role of the best man has essentially remained unchanged throughout history. A man finds a woman that he wants to marry and he needs a friend to convince him that he is doing the right thing. We men are funny that way. We demand the right to think on our own, then we get advice reassuring us that we are right. In the days of yore, however, the responsibilities of the best man were quite simple. Show up, witness the wedding, congratulate the couple (maybe unload some bullets into the air) and leave, end of story. It is only through over-excitement that weddings themselves have become elaborate affairs, demanding more of all the individuals involved.

To simplify things, here is a generalized list of the basic duties that you may (or may not) be asked to perform.

1. **Money Collector:** This entails collecting money from the other groomsmen and ushers, consulting with them, then ordering and delivering an appropriate gift from them (including yourself) to the groom. This is a big undertaking because I know how much a man hates to shop. We usually have good intentions at the outset, but end up getting so frustrated with malls and shopping plazas that we buy something inappropriate in haste. Such is the sacrifice for a friend.

This is more or less the male equivalent of the bridal shower gift. Usually any sort of gift will suffice, it doesn't necessarily have to be something specific for his new house or for him and the bride – a gift that you would appreciate receiving from your friends if you were getting married. Sporting equipment (golf clubs, baseball gear, etc.), cigars, car parts, an hour with a supermodel or a fishing cabin in the woods. All of these make great gifts, and depending on the generosity of your fellow groomsmen, you may find yourself giving him something simple, yet useful, like an electric PEZ dispenser.

2. **Clothing Coordinator:** "Hey Jimmy, are you wearing your Chicago Bulls T-shirt to school tomorrow, 'cuz I'll wear mine too okay, we'll look totally cool." Those days of clothing

coordination (or is it un-coordination) are over, so welcome to adulthood.

This task may not be delegated to you, but it is often a general best man responsibility to coordinate the clothing worn by the groomsmen and ushers.

You should call all of those involved on the groom's side together – fathers (bride's also), ushers, groomsmen and ring bearer (if male) – get all of their sizes and make sure that the rental store receives the information in plenty of time to set aside the proper clothing. Depending on the wedding, only some of these gentlemen may be expected to wear similar suits.

You should also be aware of when the groom is leaving for the honeymoon. If it is right after the wedding, you will also be responsible to return his tuxedo, and anybody else's tux, if they cannot do so on their own.

3. Packer: No, not the player from Green Bay, rather, the stuffer of clothing into the suitcase before / after the wedding for the honeymoon. I know what you are thinking: why do I have to help my friend pack for his honeymoon? What is he, an idiot or something, that he's never been on a trip before, besides, it's a honeymoon, what do you need to take other than vitamin E? Well, you would be quite surprised. People tend to forget a lot of things when they're under a lot of pressure, especially on a day like this. So it is your job to make sure that they have the essentials so that their honeymoon is as worry free as their wedding was (I hope).

4. Driver: This is actually the most important of all the best man requirements, getting the groom to the church (or wherever the wedding is taking place) on time. After you help the groom get dressed, which usually entails telling him to hurry up from in front of the TV while he dresses himself, you are to escort him to the aforementioned place of his wedding without incident.

You are under no responsibility to be the driver of the vehicle yourself and it is in fact preferred that you leave the driving in the hands of a professional. The groom may try to (and often does) convince you that he is having second thoughts. This is when having your hands unencumbered by a steering wheel comes in handy, allowing you to freely administer blows to your friend to enlighten him on how happy he is. A rented limo is the popular choice (which you take care of), because it is spacious enough in case the groom is being extra difficult. If you do drive on your own, under no circumstances are you to let the groom drive, else you may find yourself in another country and suddenly answering to the name of Pepe. A good thing about driving yourself, however, is that you are both wearing tuxedos, and on the off-chance you are speeding and get pulled over, the police are apt to let you off with a warning because of your excuse that you are late. This, of course, is no excuse to dress up in tuxedos all the time, racing around the city, because sooner or later the boys in blue will be on to you.

The key element here though is to get the man to the wedding on time (if nothing else). Just think of the emotional pressure that you have put on everybody waiting for you. The bride will think that she has been stood up, everyone in attendance will start to bad mouth your friend and you may cause the entire day to be pushed back because of timing. If this does happen you may start to think that Pepe really isn't such a bad name after all.

One more thing: if the bride and groom need a car to take them from the reception to the airport for the honeymoon, it is your responsibility to rent and return the vehicle, if such is needed.

5. Witness: This responsibility is actually the very reason why best men were invented. By law a witness is needed to prove that the wedding did indeed take place, and to sign his (or her) name stating thus.

This duty has become more of an honor than simply signing one's name. You get to stand at the side of the groom during the ceremony. He can walk down the aisle with you or just join you at the front. And you're there to prompt the groom if he forgets what to say, or remind him of the car ride if he starts to get rubber legs.

You are to be by his side the whole day, getting dressed, driving in the car and during the reception. The idea behind this is so that the groom doesn't have to feel that he is doing this alone, and that he has somebody to witness the exact time when he started to flip out and lose it. You are also there because most people tend to lose their minds at weddings, getting all hysterical, crying and stuff, and you must be calm and composed and answer any questions about the ceremony in case doubts have been raised about it later.

6. The Money Man and Wedding Police: This is another one of those responsibilities that may or may not be required of you at the wedding. Generally speaking, most weddings are paid for in advance, or days after everything has passed. However, there have been several instances when services rendered for the wedding are collected right after the festivities. Often the father of the bride or the groom (or whoever is paying) does not want to be disturbed when the procession of hands starts, awaiting their money. So they will write out several checks in advance and/or hand you a big envelope full of cash and let you appropriately deal with the details of paying the band, clergyman, caterer, waiters, bartenders, etc.

You may also be the middleman between those attending the reception and those administering it. If the bar runs out of something, they should be instructed to tell you, etc.

Another item on your growing list of responsibilities is to be the wedding police. Ideally, this responsibility is never truly enforced – I mean to say that nothing gets so out of hand that somebody has to step in to intervene, it's a wedding after all. There are those, however, directed by tradition, who aim to use the bride and groom's car as a decoration studio, letting the world know of the events that have transpired this day. Your job is to convince them that it is unsuitable for them to proceed with acts of decorative vandalism, unless you are involved in some way. After all, you are the best man.

The key thing to remember is that although it is all in fun, these pranks are usually carried out under the influence of alcohol and that they often, not properly planned in advance, may prove to be harmful.

7. Speaker: In most cases, the best man is usually expected to say at least one thing at a wedding. This will vary from wedding to wedding, but the most common speeches that you might be asked to give are: The first toast to the bride and groom, a toast to the bridesmaids, and/or reminding the guests that the cutlery belongs to the hotel. These speeches can be as long or short as you like, but should be appropriate for all those in attendance. You will try to be the wittiest, most charismatic speaker that ever orated, but you will more than likely fail. Just keep in mind the meaning and purpose of the toast and you won't have any trouble being effective.

As well as speaking at the wedding, it is often customary for the best man to be the emcee at the rehearsal dinner. This provides an excellent opportunity to roast the groom safely surrounded by a few close friends, rather than truly embarrassing him in front of all of his family and friends. You may also be asked to emcee the wedding reception.

8. Stag Master: Not all of the responsibilities that you are involved with need to be so strict and formal. This leaves the traditional stag or bachelor party, where health and chromosomal damage are secondary issues. Fun is the mainstay of all bachelor parties, and this will not stray from such long-standing traditional values if you can help it. Basically, to initiate a bachelor party, all you really need to know are the names and telephone numbers of friends of the groom that you are not already associated with and away you go.

Other Requirements

The above list constitutes the usual requirements of the best man in today's weddings. There are often several more (or sometimes fewer) things that the best man need attend to to make his best friend's wedding a success. Sometimes these responsibilities are based on a long-standing tradition, other times they are just plain silly.

☞ A tradition among Scottish fisherman is that the best man must carry the key of the brides "Kist" or hope chest over his heart and walk in procession to the groom's house, where the bride will open the chest prior to entering.

☞ It is said that the best man is to share his bed with the groom on the eve of the wedding to ensure that he doesn't get cold feet. Which is the last place I'd want to be if he did have cold feet.

☞ To convince the groom that nothing's going to change in his life after he's married (yeah, right).

☞ To discuss everything possible with the groom before the wedding, except details about the wedding.

☞ It is said that it is lucky for the bride to kiss a dirty chimney sweep in front of the family hearth. This is to be arranged by the best man, who bribes the sweep with money and a glass of beer. Good luck!

☞ Bride-stealing: Now a felony, but long ago widely accepted, the best man would kidnap the bride-to-be and hold her for ransom. The groom would have to prove himself worthy and brave and retrieve her while all of their friends and family raised the ransom money (later used for the bride and groom to build/buy a house).

☞ It was also considered very lucky if the best man and the bridesmaid of the wedding were married, or at the very least engaged. Do you see a pattern here? You agree to help your friend with his wedding and they want you to get married to the bride's best friend first because it's considered lucky.

☞ The best man and maid of honor agree to be the godparents of the newlyweds' firstborn child. Note: This decision may cause rioting amongst all the aunts and uncles still alive, so be careful that some of them aren't the spiteful types.

☞ To be the permanent, on-call babysitter for the couple's baby when nobody else is available.

☞ To constantly remind the bridesmaids during the wedding and reception how lovely they look, even if they are wearing the most hideous dresses that anybody has ever seen.

☞ To spend a night in the woods with the groom on the night before his wedding, to allow the woodland spirits to cleanse the groom for his new bride, but prevent them from taking him with them.

☞ Help the groom to slay a dragon for his bride.

☞ To maintain the groom's livelihood while he is on his honeymoon so that the couple may return without an apparent loss of income from the wedding.

☞ The best man must promise that if the groom should die within his first year of marriage, that the best man will marry his bride (in the event that the groom is without a brother to do so). If the groom should die after a year of marriage, the best man does not have to marry the woman, but must manage the deceased husband's resources to support the wife. When these resources have been depleted, this financial responsibility is to be undertaken out of his own pocket (if he hasn't already been successful in finding another husband for her). You can sense the difficulty in asking your friend to be your best man under circumstances such as these, and the reluctance of the proposed best man to accept.

Reasoning

So why are you a best man? I mean, you were picked to do the job, but why? Can you say NO? Besides, other than it being your *friend* who asked you, why should you go through with it? Obviously it is a personal decision whether to accept this honor, and you are under no pressing obligation to do so. It is ultimately your choice to accept or decline the proposal, but if you are really having trouble deciding, here are some things to consider before making a decision.

The Top Ten Reasons to become a best man.

10. All of the single women at the wedding think that your title "best" is an all-encompassing word.
9. Giving the stripper from the bachelor party the tip.
8. Pretending to lose the wedding ring at the church.
7. Free dinner.
6. Getting to embarrass your friend in front of everybody he knows.
5. You don't have to worry about finding a good seat at the reception.
4. Refusing to pay the band if they play the Macarena.
3. Signing the wedding register using a false name.

2. Blackmailing your friend using the bachelor party video that you taped.
1. Because you were asked.

With the good comes the bad, and it wouldn't be much of a book if I only showed you one side of the coin all of the time. For every positive reason there is for becoming a best man, there is bound to be a negative one.

The Top Ten Reasons not to become a best man.

10. Everybody continually reminding you that you are still single.
9. Those awful wedding dances that you're forced to endure.
8. Actually losing the ring at the church.
7. Having to cough up $5000 for a new ring.
6. Finding the wedding ring the day after you spend $5000 on a new one and not being able to get a refund because you bought it off some guy wearing a long black coat in an alley outside a bar.
5. Paying for a woman to take off all of her clothes and dance for your best friend.
4. The bride keeps trying to set you up with the maid of honor, who looks hideous in that dress of hers.
3. You still have flashbacks from wearing a tuxedo at your high-school prom.
2. Getting your butt kicked by all of the waiters because the father of the bride skipped out on the tab.
1. Being hung over for the three weeks following the stag party.

The Female Best Person

Hey, it happens, it's the 90s. Sometimes a man's best friend is a woman (next to his wife I'm sure), and he wants this woman to stand up for him at his wedding. Other times the best person is the groom's sister (particularly suitable when the groom and best person are twins).

The role for the best person is essentially identical to the role of the best man. Why change things? The only consideration that may be discussed, depending on the circumstances of the wedding party, is best person attire. So what is the proper attire? Well, for the most part, the groom, best man and ushers wear tuxedos for a formal wedding. This, however, does not mean that a tuxedo is mandatory attire if the best man is female, and in most cases it looks inappropriate.

Several sources have suggested that the best person should be attired in colors similar to that of the groom and ushers, except, of course, wearing a dress. The dress should be simple yet formal and should in no way conflict with or upstage any other dress in the bridal party, particularly the bride's. Black is usually the most common and accepted color, and should be the color of choice, wearing black nylons or stockings and black shoes. Nothing should be worn in the hair (flowers etc.) and any flashy jewelry should be avoided.

If the groom is wearing white, usually the ushers will wear gray, so the dress should be gray as well. The whole point is to blend into the wedding party, not to contrast with it, although what the etiquette is in these types of situations tends to vary. The best person should consult the bride and groom in regards to these matters, as often times a color scheme can be, and is discussed.

As you can plainly see, the responsibilities of the best man/person are fairly straightforward, although they do, and can, differ drastically from wedding to wedding. The key is to know ahead of time what is expected of you – that way there are seldom any surprises that will pop up to haunt you later.

Another key factor in undertaking any of these duties is to be prepared. It certainly doesn't hurt to read up on things, or to ask other friends for advice (providing that they have some to offer), and having done this, your friend and his bride will be eternally grateful.

Chapter Two
The Bachelor Party

The Bachelor Party can be a very difficult thing to undertake. In many relationships today, the get-drunk, party-all-night-long in the company of naked professionals is frowned upon. Then there is the overwhelming sense of tradition that draws us towards overlooking this disapproval, often jeopardizing the very reason we are celebrating. It really depends on how much influence the best man has and how prepared he is to cover up the dirty tracks. By no means do I mean that deceit should play a hand in any of this. After all, the institution of marriage is not to be taken lightly, especially with a hooker on your arm. So, for the sake of all parties involved, we will discuss as many traditions, ideas, themes, extremities and abnormalities as possible to encompass the entire gamut that represents the Bachelor Party.

Party professionals

Where does one begin when organizing a bachelor party? Quite simply, turn to the professionals. Now I don't mean *those* professionals, I mean the ones that organize parties for a living, and let's face it, when it comes to organizing these types of things, men don't want to bother. That's why there are individuals or companies who offer their services for just such occasions.

One of the great benefits of hiring somebody to do the work for you is that it saves you a lot of time and effort as well as providing you with a well-organized party that you can take all of the credit for. That's why you bought this book. You needed help.

Another great benefit of using outside help is that they will do a much better job than you can on your own. It's not that we are idiots and can't muddle our way through it so that everybody is happy – of course we can. The big picture is that this party represents something important to you and your best friend the groom, and you'll want to make it something truly memorable for him (and you).

These companies, or individuals, take care of all of the details for you and usually at a fairly reasonable price, so it doesn't have to cost you an arm or a leg. They provide everything for you, from arranging transportation, making dinner reservations and providing set menu selections, organizing various events (sporting, theatre), booking facilities (reception halls, cabins, boats, buses), getting entertainment (bands, dancers, clowns, dealers), setting up games and activities, flights and hotels, etc.

They will then give you a per person cost for all of this (depending on what you want) with their fee worked into this quote as well. They will then offer you an itinerary to follow, but usually accompany you as the driver/coordinator to make sure there are no problems with any of the details (of course, a tip is usually offered to this person at the end, in addition to their regular fee).

I have solicited the help of these professionals on a number of occasions, not only for stag parties, but also for company outings, etc. I find them very professional and reliable, but it all depends on the reputation of the company. I have also found that an average organized outing with dinner (wine included) and entertainment runs about $50-100 per person (additional alcohol is extra). This all depends on several factors and what everybody is willing to spend. The best thing to do is to find out from everybody attending what they are willing to spend and approach the organizer with this budget to work with, and they will provide you with a party to meet that budget.

If you hire someone to help you, even if it's just a friend with great organizing capabilities, make sure they know what you want up front. That way there is no confusion about your plans when the time comes. I also find that if you and your friends continually use one of these individuals or companies, not only does the price get better, but so does the entertainment that you get for your dollar.

Party ideas

There are several different ways you can undertake a bachelor or stag party on your own, and it all really depends on the time and resources available to you. Ideally, every groom would love it if his best man got everybody together for a weekend in Vegas, but alas, such is never the case. (For those already living in Vegas, this really isn't such a thrill; perhaps they would fly to Canada or something).

The whole idea behind the bachelor party is to give the groom one last chance to enjoy being single. You want to remind him of what he is missing; and to propel him head-long into the waiting arms of his bride-to-be (with a pounding headache, and no reservations about the institution of marriage whatsoever).

You'll want to make the party different from the usual weekends that you already spend with him and the boys, going out and getting drunk. Make it different, make it exciting, stir things up a little bit.

The following list contains several ideas for theme parties or outings that often provide something a little different from your usual boys' night out.

1. The cabin

What could be better than getting together with all of your friends at a quiet, secluded spot in the middle of nowhere? Sure, rent a cabin near a lake and get all of your buddies together for a day or two.

☞ Set up a scavenger hunt for the drive down to pass the time. It really makes the trip much more eventful.

☞ At the cabin take everybody's watch and car keys away. Not being able to tell the time, you eat when you are hungry and sleep when you are tired. And if some of your friends start complaining that they miss their wives or their girlfriends, too bad, because nobody can leave 'till it's all over.

☞ Have a television set and a VCR available to play video-tapes (movies, sports or material illegal in most states).

☞ Bring along a camcorder to record things for posterity (also good to show later at the wedding or as proof to the bride that everything was harmless, or use the tape to blackmail the groom [what's a little extortion between friends?]).

☞ Make sure there is plenty of food and beverages. There's bound to be a lot of eating and drinking, so be prepared. Make sure that your location isn't so remote that you can't re-stock up on supplies, especially if you are staying for more than one day. Also have a variety of food – sure, you can all get by on 20 gallons of chili and two dozen hotdogs each, but it's nice to have a choice too.

☞ Have a fishing contest and give prizes (not having to clean the fish or do the dishes), or have various sporting events (baseball, water skiing, volleyball or my personal favorite, football).

☞ Play card games (poker) or board games (poker with dice). If you decide to involve money in these games, have a rule that a percentage goes to the bride and groom (but that shouldn't be an excuse for the groom to try and bleed everyone dry).

☞ Although I usually don't recommend this as a popular or safe choice, under the care of responsible individuals, you could always go hunting. When I think of my friends in this case, a bunch of drinking fools with firearms does not paint a safe picture in my mind. We'll probably end up trying to shoot the groom and get him stuffed, pre-senting him to his bride-to-be, all stiff and full of straw. However, again, for those with self-control, this is cer-tainly a suitable choice for an activity.

☞ If you don't have access to a cabin, go camping instead. All of the above factors still apply, except now, you get to do them all outdoors.

There are a number of great things that you can do while spending time at a cabin. The idea is to get away for a while to be with your friends and the man you are honoring. It is certainly much better than going to the same-old place, and doing the same-old things, even if it is only a select few that attend.

2. The golf tourney

Who says that bachelor parties have to take place at night? The golf tourney is a great way to get everybody together for the day. A golf tournament promises a day filled with competition, driving the ball down the fairway, trying to outdo your friends, usually plastered out of your mind. Even if you're not a great golfer, it's a lot of fun. The following represents some things that you should take care of when organizing such an event for friends.

☞ Be aware of tee off times – on a nice day it may be difficult to book an early time. You may be better off going to a more modest course, because you will probably have a better chance of getting a large group booked.

☞ Contact the course well in advance to book the course as a large group and be sure to ask what kind of discount you can qualify for.

☞ Find out everybody's handicap and make up fair teams (it keeps things competitive).

☞ Collect the money from all of your friends, plus a little surplus for those unexpected expenses that pop up.

☞ Try to arrange prizes, and offer them for the longest drive, best score, closest to the pin, longest putt sunk, as well as most balls lost, worst slice (or would that be best slice?) and worst score. Your friends might be able to help out, depending on their jobs, by offering some prizes, or simply get everybody to chip in a little bit more money and buy something with that.

☞ Arrange rests and beverages for the course, but keep in mind the course rules on how they like to handle this sort of thing.

☞ If you are making this a full day thing, as it usually turns out with a large group, try to arrange something with the course restaurant and clubhouse, to eat and drink after you are done.

☞ Don't forget that camcorder for posterity, etc.

☞ Solicit the aid of somebody at the golf course to organize all of this for you. They usually have somebody in PR or sales that does this kind of thing. That way all you have to do is to give them a list of names and an envelope of cash.

Once again, the idea behind this event is to get everybody together doing something as a group, that way nobody leaves feeling bored. It also provides a great way for people to meet one another, particularly if all of the men attending the party are not from the same circle of friends. What it also does is allow several of the older individuals, who usually forego attending a drunk nudie-fest, the chance to attend the bachelor party and enjoy themselves. Invite anyone and everyone.

3. War games

Nothing quite separates the men from the boys during a stag party like having your face covered with camouflage paint and shooting at all of your friends from behind some trees. Actually it's a great way for everybody to get rid of all of that pent-up energy before you watch the stripper dance. Of course, you have to make sure that you do not have any enemies among your friends, or that none of your friends start acting strange once they have a gun in their hands. They are usually easy to spot. They stare at you with a crooked smile on their face and mumble to themselves. If you have a friend like this in your group, let him be the one that goes to get the beer, while everybody else plays.

Another great thing about playing war games is that it can be done at any time of the day, and is often available both indoors and out (in case it rains, but then again, that's half the fun). Things to remember:

☞ Try to be on the same side as the groom. Although he is always the first one targeted, sympathy for his up-coming nuptials often prevails, and his team is given a mercy win.

☞ Try to avoid being near the groom while playing since he will be heavily pelted with paint pellets (and often by members of the same team who blame the "accident" on their defective weapon). The whole idea is to shoot him so often that you leave little welts on his body, thus returning him lumpy to his bride. You will want to remind him that his best option is death, rather than marriage, but you will have to settle for paint staining his body one shot at a time because he simply refuses to listen.

☞ Make reservations well in advance, and make sure that lunch/food is offered.

☞ Collect money from your friends in advance.

☞ Don't wear clothes you want to keep. It can get very dirty and messy sometimes, and the market seems to be void of any laundry detergent that uses the slogan "Great for the stains caused by war." Also wear decent shoes/boots – you'll probably be in the dirt and mud, which is never fun with really wet feet.

☞ Douse yourself in insect repellent, especially if you are going to be playing outdoors. The facility may offer several field modes (i.e., dry, wet or swampy), and mosquitoes like nothing better than to breed in small pools of stagnant water. Besides, you won't always be running at full speed (where the mosquitoes can't catch you) screaming "*charge*" at the top of your lungs. Nobody fights like that anymore, but if you do, be prepared to be out of the game quickly.

☞ Make sure that protective ear gear is supplied, otherwise bring your own. Hey, you know how the saying goes: "It's all fun and games until somebody loses an eye . . . then it's a sport!"

☞ Try to use only non-hypoallergenic camouflage paint because . . . (I'm kidding).

4. "Condom head" and "The old ball and chain"

Oh, I'm sure that you've seen them available at any novelty shop, or seen some other boob wearing one, embarrassed in public by his friends. These little party favors are perfect for the groom who likes to attract attention, and be ridiculed for it (or one who hates attention for that matter). But what do you care, he's getting married, he won't have anything to be embarrassed about anymore, so you might as well make this one good.

☞ Make sure that your plans include taking the groom out in public. Having him wear any of these things just in the company of his friends is redundant, because they've all seen him embarrassed before. It stops being funny after about twenty minutes unless complete strangers get to laugh at him too.

☞ Make dinner reservations at a fancy restaurant. Nothing impresses high priced places, or their guests, quite like a bunch of loud guys cheering and praising the condom king.

☞ The only thing that truly accomodates a man wearing a big rubber condom on his head is a bust cake (so named because it resembles the torso of a naked woman). Again, a fancy restaurant is a great place for this, and almost every baker that has ever lived dreams of creating a cake like this. In the event that you simply cannot get the cake made, which is impossible because I've had supermarket bakeries make them for me, then you'll have to settle for a real woman covered in frosting.

☞ To further disgust the masses (no, really, it's disgusting, but it has been done), equip everybody attending the stag party with water pistols filled with cream (or hand lotion) for that full condom head effect. I'll forego the visual description of how you might offer praise to the Condom King, as I'm sure you can guess on your own.

☞ Tie lifesavers on the groom's shirt with thread and tape a sign on his back – "A-buck-a-suck" – and put the dollar that he makes towards his honeymoon. (Although I know of somebody that managed to make over $30, and had to go out and buy additional packages of candy because he kept running out). People (hopefully women) are supposed to find the groom irresistible and pay him a dollar to suck/bite a candy off his shirt.

☞ If you are using the "ball and chain" gag, be sure to use a plastic version. I've heard of stories where they used a real ball and chain and:

1. The metal brace started to cut through his ankle.

2. Somebody misplaced the key and they had to call a locksmith, or a locksmith wasn't available and they ended up using a hacksaw to free the groom.

3. The groom dropped it on his foot and broke three of his toes.

4. Many an establishment has insisted that they be reimbursed because the heavy metal ball has caused damage to their floor tiles.

☞ To fully make the ball and chain more memorable, have a picture of the bride-to-be painted, or pasted, on the ball. This serves not only to remind the groom what it represents, but also to allow unknowing strangers the opportunity to sympathize with the lucky girl that gets to marry this clown.

☞ Bring magic markers and write on him (the permanent kind, so it takes him a week of scrubbing to come clean).

☞ Let him write on you (the non-permanent kind so that you can wash it off before going to bed without the fear of staining your sheets).

5. Take me out to the ball game

Why make things all complicated and difficult to organize and plan? Just keep things simple. A bunch of friends enjoying a day at the ballpark, or football field, hockey arena (whatever). What could be better than watching professional athletes performing for your enjoyment, and having a couple of brew and some dogs?

☞ Book tickets in advance so that everybody can get seats together. The arena/diamond usually offers group discounts, and be sure to collect the money from your friends in advance or else you may find yourself scalping tickets before the game just to break even. You can also try to see if you can book a corporate box for the game, that way they provide food and beverages and it's a little bit more private for you so that you can freely mingle and talk.

☞ Bring banners supporting your favorite team, including the bride's and groom's names for full effect.

☞ Arrange to have your friend's name (and/or your group's purpose) announced between innings/periods/half time, and maybe if you're lucky, the game is being televised and they will zoom in on your location and you'll all get to be on television.

☞ For those hard core stag/sport lovers, paint your bodies in support of the sport and your friend's upcoming wedding. You're sure to attract attention and (as above) get your group on television.

☞ If you have any connections whatsoever at the stadium/arena, you can try to have the groom-to-be sing the national anthem before the game.

The great thing about attending a sporting event is the entertainment is already provided. It is also very seldom that someone has a bad time at one of these events. What it also does is allow an all-encompassing invitation list (i.e., fathers, boys, clergy), because again, the more the merrier. Ideally, to accommodate all of the seating, arrange groups of four seats across several rows. That way your party is not strung out so far that the people on either end cannot communicate with anybody else. Place the groom right in the center of everything, so that anyone can talk to him.

6. River rafting and house boating

Since both of these stag party choices involve water, I want to stress that the proper care should be taken when undertaking one of these adventures, especially if alcohol is involved. Similar to the cabin, these trips/outings offer the opportunity for the group to get away for the day to be together (or several days depending on the planning).

House boating allows ample opportunity to move the party around from place to place (or town to town), stopping to swim, relax, dock and party. It also provides a great venue for activities, fishing, sightseeing and poker (much like the old river boat casinos).

☞ Book well in advance and prepare yourself in the event of rain (activities indoors, etc.). You will probably have to put a deposit down to reserve the boat(s); make sure that it is refundable in case your plans change.

☞ Avoid renting a houseboat on the Niagara River (near Niagara Falls). Many a happy day has ended in tragedy with the last words "wow, she's really starting to pick up speed now, I didn't know these things went this fast. By the way, what's that loud noise?"

☞ Put somebody responsible in charge of driving. Running these things aground can get expensive. When you're not cruising around, use the anchor.

☞ Make sure that you are well stocked-up with food and beverages, or that there is access to go ashore and stock up as required.

☞ Have maps (and an understanding of how to read them) of the water system that you are on as well as of the surrounding area, and any stops along your travel route. Plan possible routes to travel along and areas to stop at to relax or disembark.

☞ Find out if there is anybody attending that doesn't know how to swim, and make sure that an ample supply of life vests is provided when you pick up the boat. "Hey, everybody look at Mike, flapping his arms all around like that in the water. Somebody throw him another beer."

River rafting is another great release from the mundane traditionalism of drinking beer and watching a peeler gear down (and really, for many men, this is already a part of our everyday lives), and something like river rafting helps to break up the monotony. Since river rafting is not always available in all areas, travel might be involved as well as camping out, so be prepared for this contingency.

☞ Ensure that the company offering the river rafting is run by professionals, all of which not only know what they are doing, but also the river or waterway they are doing it on. Sometimes students are hired who are not fully aware of all of the dangers, and that's the last thing you need to worry about.

☞ Find out what kinds of things are included in the price (food, tents, transportation back up the river, etc.) so that you can work out a per person cost and know what other expenses you will be responsible for.

☞ Find out what they offer in the way of off-time activities. In other words, what you can do when you're not on the river, or what there is to do at night (if it is a multi-day outing).

☞ Remember that video camera to capture those surprised looks (or scared stiff looks) on everybody's faces when they travel down the river.

7. Pub-crawls

Note: This should only be attempted for those not worried about possible chromosomal damage.

> **Pub-crawl:** To drink to the point where the only way the body can transport itself from one place to another is by crawling on one's hands and knees. This is the preferred position to be in for several reasons:

1. It provides an eye level of the toilet bowl, where you will probably be spending the night.

2. When your brain finally shuts itself off, trying desperately to retain enough brain cells for the more important functions like breathing, you only have a short distance to fall to the floor.

3. It takes us back to our childhood, which is what drinking alcohol often does. When we were babies we would often stumble around in our underwear with a bottle in our hands (what a coincidence). Our only way to get anywhere was on our hands and knees (another coincidence).

The pub-crawl, the very backbone of being drunk and disorderly, is a long-standing tradition taking men back to their college/university days, and even further back to their ancestry, when their forefathers would swill grog at several of the local taverns before setting out to behead their foes in battle. Not much has changed from those earlier days, except of course the beheading part, which has basically been whittled down to idle threats at best.

How does one organize a pub-crawl? Well, this complex system must be followed with the strictest goals in mind. One deviation from the parent plan can lead to devastating results. The following represents a detailed summary of everything that should be committed to memory prior to undertaking an evening of pub-crawling.

1. Rent a bus and a driver.
2. Arrange a number of pubs to visit (calling ahead to avoid the line ups).
3. Grab a beer, lift and drink.
4. Repeat step 3.

There are several other things that you may want to do so that this evening will be fully appreciated.

☞ Have T-shirts made up (e.g., "Billy's Stag") for everybody attending the stag. That way you won't lose anybody and they'll act as a beacon when you're hammered out of your mind. You'll be able to turn to the guy on the floor next to you and say "hey, I know you" just by looking at his shirt.

☞ Give the driver a list of everybody's names and addresses so that he/she can keep tabs on everybody, so that nobody is left behind. This is also great at the end of the night when people need to be dropped off at home and are too drunk to remember where they live.

☞ Because you're in a large group, arrange with certain pubs that you plan to visit to have snacks available (to help to absorb some of the alcohol). That way you won't start losing participants by the first pub.

☞ If you can operate a video camera, bring one along. Although what usually happens is that the first few hours of tape are fine, but by the end of the night your blurry vision becomes evident on the recording you are making, or you end up with long spanning shots of the carpet from a floor level view.

8. Road trips

Road trips are the essential tool in maintaining a man's sanity. Sometimes we just need to pack up and get away from everything for a couple of days (or even just one day), and we want to bring a friend (or 20) along to help us to forget why we are escaping our problems. Now don't confuse the "Road Trip" with "running away," although they are similar to an extent. The primary reason for the road trip is that you are getting away from the same old places and the same old faces. So you go for a drive to another place where you are essentially a stranger, and you won't run into anybody to whom you owe money. This differs from running away, for the simple fact that you will return as soon as your money runs out, or the alcohol wears off (whichever comes first).

Let's face it, we're men and we don't tend to organize things very well, but we can all drive. (Bear with me, there is a point in here someplace). Since a stag party represents a form of organization, we will probably tire of it very soon unless it is something we can do with minimal effort. But, we want to have fun with all of our friends too, and so we drive.

There's something about being packed on a bus that brings men together, to bond as friends. It's like going to that big game in high school, as a team. Or heading off to training camp in the army. Even getting your butt carted off to prison, being crammed on a bus with the rest of society's scourge, brings you together, despising authority and collective against the man.

I'm not really sure if any of these reasons truly apply, but we still enjoy it all the same.

☞ Rent a bus, because nobody will want to sacrifice having fun to be the responsible one to do all of the driving.

☞ Don't be overly concerned if you get lost. Men always get lost, and our egos prevent us from asking for directions, so instead of losing face, blame it on the driver and relax.

☞ Take lots of pictures or a video, you may need it as proof of where you've been.

☞ Create a false identity. If there is one thing that people in small towns like, it's to be tricked. And if you're really good at it, you may even convince your friends by the end of the trip.

☞ Have a destination in mind before you depart. Nobody likes driving aimlessly around searching for apparently nothing (unless of course you are a bunch of teenage boys, then this is usually the high point of your day).

☞ Don't give the groom access to a phone (unless you have been incarcerated).

9. Hunting and gathering

For you die hard, back to nature, back to the stone-age, aggressive types, there is a more primitive choice, taking you back to your roots, using nothing but sheer instinct, and the thrill of the hunt. What you decide to do is really up to you, but here are a few tips if you are having trouble getting started.

☞ Read *Lord of the Flies* to get yourself in the primitive mood.

☞ Strip down to your underwear and cover yourself with war paint, camouflage paint or whatever your girlfriend/wife has laying around the bathroom.

☞ Find a small, uninhabited island (as this provides the best effect), but you can also use a park or a field (generally away from someone who might think you deranged and have you arrested). A neighborhood backyard can also provide ample effect (for those urban dweller types of hunters and gatherers).

☞ Rent and watch the movie "Quest for Fire" strictly for those guttural sounds that will make up most of your vocabulary during this adventure. (**Note:** If this movie is not available, mimic Tim Allen from "Home Improvement").

☞ Find something to hunt (this is where the island really adds that primitive touch). If there really isn't anything wild to hunt (apart from rats and squirrels), plastic antlers, a dog and some duct tape is quite effective, but be careful that whatever you do hunt will not be missed by its owner.

☞ Hunt and Gather. Teamwork is the key here. Even though it appears to be a run-of-the-mill pet, it's the emotion that surrounds it that makes it dangerous. They are still chock full of animal instincts, especially when they are continually prodded with hot dog forks, and it may require the entire group to bring it down. This is when the aid of a professional really gets things going (somebody from animal control, a teacher, butcher or lawyer).

☞ If you simply can't find a live animal to hunt, there's always plenty of fresh meat at the local Pay-N-Save. It defeats the hunting part of things, but it sure makes the gathering part a whole lot easier.

10. Traditionalism

Last but certainly not least, I bring you the long-standing bachelor tradition, strippers and beer. Now I apologize if this section comes off as being sexist in any way, shape or form. I am merely transcribing information on a long-standing tradition to the reader, and how you interpret it is your problem.

The long-standing tradition that I speak of in this case requires a large group of stag party attendees to be entertained by the removal of clothing from an attractive woman with an outstanding body – a stripper, in other words.

Before embarking on this road, however, the discerning best man must be aware of the repercussions that this evening may bring forth. Usually, the bride-to-be fully trusts her husband-to-be and such factors don't come into play in your entertainment scheme. But, many a starting relationship such as this is not totally founded on trust at this early stage, and care must be taken not to jeopardize this fact. After all, is an evening of nude dancing worth losing a life long partner over?

If you do proceed with this traditional form of entertainment, there are several factors that you should keep in mind.

☞ Discretion

☞ Collect the money from your friends in advance.

☞ If you are having dinner first, prepare plenty of time to eat before the entertainment arrives. Many a meal has gotten cold because of poor timing, and as men, our priority is such that "Amber" falls higher on the list than eating.

☞ Ensure that wherever it is that you will be entertained, that it will not interfere with the business of the establishment you're in. If you're already in a strip club, this is not a factor. However, family restaurants tend to frown on naked women dancing on one of their tables in the middle of the dining room.

☞ No cameras allowed. Just in case the stripper embarrasses the groom, we certainly don't want a reminder of it on film.

☞ No weak-willed sissies allowed.

☞ Don't pay the stripper in advance (prior to showing up); pay her once she has performed her obligation, and ensure you know how long she will dance, etc., first. At the very least, to protect her interests, half before, half after is often acceptable.

☞ If you plan other festivities prior to the floorshow, don't get too drunk too fast or the entertainment might not be so visually stimulating.

☞ When arranging to hire the dancer from an agency, ask to meet her in person rather than simply seeing her picture. Pictures can be old and/or time has a way of changing a person's appearance. Many a stag party has been criticized because the dancer looked nothing like her picture, and the bottom line comes down to your hiring capabilities.

☞ Always have a back up plan. In other words, the dancer might not show, the restaurant you are having dinner in doesn't allow this type of entertainment, etc.

☞ If you intend for a lot of alcohol to be involved, make sure to set up a designated driver.

☞ If you are having dinner first, make the necessary dinner reservations well in advance, and confirm them a few times. Also try to inform the restaurant if there are any changes, i.e., additional/fewer people in the party, if you are going to be late, etc.

☞ When you arrange to hire the stripper, don't use your real name (hey, she's not using her real name, why should you?). I like to use my boss's name for such occasions – in fact, I often carry several copies of his business card just for these circumstances.

It is obvious that you will more than likely enjoy yourself, just make sure that it doesn't get out of hand. These women are certainly professionals, however, they are still human beings just like the rest of us, and they're just trying to make a living, so don't overlook that fact for the sake of tradition.

Other activities

The following is a partial list of other things that you may want to try/embark on for your bachelor party. Several of them are tried and tested stag hits, but in the end it is your decision. I hope that this gives you some different ideas.

☞ A bowling tournament

☞ Billiards (rent a small billiards hall, order pizza and beer, and set up a tournament)

☞ Go-Cart or Mini-Indy car racing

☞ Group massages

☞ Rent a hall, book a band, sell tickets (proceeds to the happy couple)

☞ Put on a bachelor benefit party (as above, except offer dinner with a per plate charge)

☞ The old-fashioned house party. Who says a stag party has to be just the guys? (Invite the neighbors, have them bring gifts).

☞ Bungee jumping

☞ A day at the ranch/farm (horseback riding)

☞ A day of hiking/rock climbing.

☞ Start a fire/put one out (just kidding)

☞ Arrange for everybody to go on a tour of the local brewery/winery.

☞ Fake arrest gag. Have the groom thrown in jail and collect the bail money from all of his family and friends for the bride and groom to use on their house/honeymoon.

☞ Hot air ballooning.

☞ A day at the beach (volleyball, surfing)

☞ A pool party

☞ Hot-tubbing

☞ Rent a chalet and go skiing for the day

☞ Jet skiing/ snow mobiling

Bachelor party blues

There have been, as I'm quite sure you are aware, several bachelor parties that have ended in disaster. Many of these occasions started off with the best intentions at heart, but for whatever reasons, turned ugly. The following stories represent such instances.

Reminder . . .

One bachelor party I attended was in full swing before mishap entered into things. The groom was certainly being entertained. They had all gone to an afternoon baseball game to start things off, where very much draft beer was consumed. After the game, they had dinner to sober up the groom, and it seemed to work. They had further entertainment arranged in a local hall where they had set up some poker tables, etc., to fill out the rest of the evening. Then at about ten o'clock additional entertainment arrived in the form of a professional dancer. The woman started to dance, the groom was poised in his chair watching intently, but the rest of the crowd couldn't see anything. They wanted to watch the groom's reaction to the naked woman in front of him, but also to see the nudity as well. Finally the best man suggested putting several tables together to make a stage to elevate the groom and the dancer so that everybody could see them. The groom sat elevated in his chair with the dancer sprawling her body before him.

The dancing continued until she was totally naked, at which time she went to sit on his lap and give him a big kiss. Well, I guess at some time during all of the dancing, some of the tables had spread slightly apart, and when the dancer sat on his lap the leg of the chair he was sitting on found its way into one of these gaps. The couple immediately found their way to the floor below, 60 staring eyes not sure whether to laugh or cry.

Needless to say, two things happened because of this incident. The first was that the best man had to pay more money than he thought imaginable to see a naked dancer do a back-flip, and the second was that the groom participated in the wedding ceremony wearing a cast on his arm. The stories that circulated about this night were repeated several times, but one good thing to come out of all of it was that the groom was left with the signed cast as a momento from his wedding day.

Reactions . . .

Another bachelor party that I organized myself brought interesting obstacles with it. Most of the people attending the party were rather a rambunctious lot and the groom, after many years of giving in to this attitude on life, straightened up his act, found a wonderful woman and was about to be married. Included in his new image was his refusal to drink alcohol anymore, a truly wonderful metamorphosis.

So how does one organize a party for 20 to 30 men, all of whom drink and party, and the only one that doesn't partake is the man of honor. Well, we let everybody do what they felt they had to do to enjoy themselves. We all went golfing that afternoon, some starting to party early, others refraining 'till dinner. Some of the guys felt that since the groom had quit drinking, it didn't seem quite like fun unless he joined them in a drink. Several of them tried repeatedly, every time they had a shooter, to force him to drink one, but he always refused. On one of these refusals, however, the drink was accidentally dumped into his lap. You never know when these things can get out of hand, and the groom didn't protest, he himself having done some outrageous things at other bachelor parties.

After dinner I had arranged for a stripper to dance for the groom. It was harmless enough. The restaurant where we had dinner had a closed off party area for us to dine in, to avoid disturbing other guests, and it also provided us with a room in which to be entertained. The stripper arrived and I chatted with her in regards to her routine, and everything seemed perfect.

The dancer put on one exciting performance. She even used some silly foam, which is essentially moldable children's foam that comes in a can. With this she bathed the groom's lap in the foam and constructed phallic towers with it. She then began to gesture intentions and ended up plopping herself into his lap, grinding this foam into his pants. Well, little did we realize that this particular brand of foam had two effects on the groom. One was that, combined with the alcohol already in his lap, it stained his pants green – not a big problem. The other was that he had some sort of allergic reaction to the chemicals that he was wearing and it stained his skin with red spots for three days. I was extremely apologetic, as was the dancer when I called her to suggest that she avoid using the product in this manner in the future.

Busted . . .

Unfortunately, this is a true story submitted by a friend.
William had done a wonderful job so far making all of the arrangements for the bachelor party. He had confirmed all those who were to attend, booked the golf course, complete with dinner afterwards at the clubhouse and he even arranged for a little stimulating entertainment to be offered in the open banquet hall of the country club. It all seemed perfect.

Everybody was having a wonderful time that day. The golfing weather was spectacular, and William even took credit for that. Dinner was equally enjoyable, the club even offered complimentary wine for the stag party because we were being so well behaved. All that remained was the dancer.

By the time the dancer arrived, several of us had been drinking for most of the day, and that, combined with the wine at dinner, put us all in festive spirits. She was simply fantastic, and not only did she dance, she had a little surprise for the groom, paid for by the best man William. A kind of oral presentation, as it were, to remind him of the end of his bachelor life.

It seems that although all of the necessary precautions had been taken, they were still not enough to avoid an incident. Somehow Sandra, the lovely bride-to-be, got word of this "oral presentation." Despite all of the saving arguments from William and several others in attendance, absolving Scott the groom of any wrongdoing, and putting the blame on themselves and Scott's drunken state, she still called off the wedding.

Busted part 2 . . .

This story, also submitted by a friend, just goes to show you how the best-laid plans can sometimes fall apart in front of your very eyes.

The groom Marshall was adamant that Steve, his best man, take all necessary precautions in making sure that whatever debaucheries he had planned for the bachelor party, it would be impossible for Debbie to find out about them. Things of late with them had been rather tense because Debbie had found out about an affair that Marshall had had several years prior when they first started going out, and she was equally adamant that no strippers, or the like, were to be involved.

Steve reassured Marshall, who reassured Debbie several times that everything was okay. First they were to have dinner at their favorite restaurant. Then they were to proceed to the Pub, where at midnight all of the girls were to meet them. The girls were having their wedding shower on the same night, and decided that they should all meet up afterwards, to keep an eye on their men, so to speak.

It all seemed harmless enough. Of course, Steve failed to mention the small detour after dinner to go to a club to watch strippers dance. But again, it was harmless enough, or so they thought, because there was no way for Debbie to find out that they were there.

When midnight rolled around, the girls showed up and the pub was in full swing. Everybody was drinking and dancing, in fact, all seemed to be well. It was at about this time that the evening crashed and burned.

Arriving late to the pub and to Debbie's shower party was her friend Sharon, who couldn't make it to the party, but agreed to meet them at the pub after she had gotten off work. It was truly unfortunate that Sharon happened to be a bartender at the strip club where the men were entertained earlier that evening, and through no fault of her own, made mention of this fact openly in front of Debbie.

To say that Debbie was furious would be an understatement. She did, however, proceed with her marriage to Marshall as planned, and the wedding took place without Steve as the best man.

Marshall and Steve are still good friends, it's just that Steve isn't allowed to visit or call his friend without Debbie causing him a great deal of grief.

Busted part 3 . . .

For a change of pace, the guys decided to spend an afternoon skiing up at the local resort in lieu of a drunken stag gathering. This way, they thought, they could enjoy a day of skiing and an evening in the chalet eating and relaxing. This idea was so welcomed that in fact most, if not all, of Randy's friends gladly attended, including myself.

The afternoon found everybody skiing together, but this quickly broke off into smaller groups, mostly based on skiing ability.

Randy was a novice skier at best, but he stuck with Adam, his best man, because they had often gone skiing together, and Randy was confident of Adam's abilities and felt that he was learning from them.

Like many sports, as the day progresses, coupled with a peer of better ability, so too does your ability improve. In fact, Randy was feeling so confident that he wanted to try some more difficult runs (black diamonds). Since it was his stag, the guys in the group, all being better skiers, agreed.

They started off on the more simple of the runs and Randy seemed to be mastering the quick turns and moguls with ease – well, to his best ability anyhow. So we went to an all-mogul run.

Many of the guys had breezed their way down the slope while Adam and Randy lagged behind a little, Adam offering tips to the novice. After a while of this, Randy, seeing that he was holding the others up, insisted that Adam proceed without him, that he would just take it slow and make his own way down. Besides, he added that this was the only was he was going to learn.

At the bottom of the run, Adam urged the others on while he waited for Randy to make his way down. Randy proceeded slowly but was making progress in short spurts of speed, only to stop abruptly or fall

*to decrease his speed. Adam laughed several times to himself. It was
at this point that Randy, now back in motion, managed to get around
a few moguls and was starting to pick up speed. In fact, he was starting
to lose control and inevitably wiped himself out.*

*Unfortunately, though, he was to one side of the run, and it was
rather icy from the fluctuations in weather from the past few days.
Randy was tumbling down this icy area and couldn't seem to stop
himself in spite of his efforts to dig his skis into the snow. Finally Randy
took flight off of the end of a big mogul and covered his head and crashed
into one of the trees lining the slope. Adam immediately screamed out
to him to see if he was okay, and then proceeded to the bottom of the
hill for help.*

*Randy had hit the tree with his upper thigh and wedged himself
under some branches (the hill being steep combined with the angle of
the tree), but in time managed to free himself.*

*On the way up the chair lift, Adam screamed to Randy to shake the
tree that he was in, so that they could get an approximate fix on his
location. Once he made it down to Randy's location on the slope, he
soon found himself face to face with his friend, laying in the snow.*

*Adam almost burst out laughing at the sight of Randy sitting there
on the face of the slope. Randy, who had been wearing sunglasses when
he hit the tree, and now was without them, had perfect raccoon eyes
where the glasses once were, and where all of the debris from the tree
fell onto his face upon impact. But he was all right. His hip had
absorbed the majority of the hit, and he felt that he would suffer with
a charley horse at best.*

*They collected his gear, which was strewn across the mountainside.
How some of it got to where they found it, I am not certain, and we
spent the rest of the afternoon drinking toddies and relaxing in front
of the fire.*

*The next day Randy woke up rather stiff, with minor pain, and thus
refrained from seeing a doctor. Several days after (5 to be exact), on
the advice of his worried mother and bride-to-be, he finally went to seek
medical attention. He argued that his leg, although tender, was free of
bruising or swelling, and that if there had been anything broken, such
wouldn't be the case. He also added that the femur was the size of a 2"
X 4" piece of wood, and that his impact with the tree was not severe
enough to cause such damage.*

*He was right, his leg was not broken, his kneecap was. It seems that
even though he hit the tree with his upper leg, the impact caused his
leg to snap at such force that it broke his kneecap right in half.*

*Randy wore a stovepipe leg cast for eight weeks, including to his
wedding. In all honesty there wasn't a funnier sight than watching
Randy in his tuxedo with one pant leg missing, at the church in front*

of everybody, having to stop every few minutes to relieve the itching under his cast by using a long stick to scratch himself.

If you managed to live through the bachelor party and there are no outstanding warrants for your arrest, consider yourself on your way to the best man Hall-of-fame. But really, the bachelor party is a very important event in a man's life, and as a friend, you have proved yourself exactly that, a friend, giving the groom something to remember from his days with his buddies. Of course, convincing him to go through with the wedding after all that has happened is still another story.

Chapter Three
The Groom

You ask yourself "Self, why am I doing this?" Then you remember, "because he is my best friend." There was a reason you were asked to represent the groom on this occasion. He trusts you to be there for him. You do this for him because you want to stand up for the person that you believe in and care for, but this doesn't have to be the only reason. It is truly an honor to be the best man at somebody's wedding, let alone someone to whom you are close.

The groom, "silly fool" you think to yourself. Still the single messenger of your gender, or the wise married owl knowledgeable in the ways of matrimony: both full of advice with which you are waiting to shower the groom. So green is your friend, unknowing what lays ahead for him, or what he is leaving behind. As his friend, you probably want to remind him of both, you know, just to intensify the confusion and anxieties that he may be feeling, or to loosen the stoicism that he proudly displays. After all, you are his friend and that's what friends do. But let us not forget the importance of the situation here, putting aside all selfishness and getting down to the heart of the matter, literally, him.

The groom can often be a difficult person to get along with; you know because you've probably been his best friend for a long time now. Now that he is getting married, his stress/tension level is probably on the rise and he may not be the easiest character to deal with. This is the main reason why you should be there for him, to ease the burden of the big day. Keeping him drunk for two or three weeks before the wedding helps, although his liver never really appreciates the full spectrum of what you were trying to accomplish, so I suggest you totally disregard that last comment.

What should you be doing? There are no specific guidelines that dictate protocol in this circumstance. He is your friend and you will be best suited to offer advice, etc., based on your long-standing friendship with him and no book can fully offer the kind of specific advice needed to help him get through this wonderful, confusing, difficult time in his life. Just being his friend at these times is often enough. Other times, it is never enough, and you really have to push your friendship to the limit to help keep things on a sane level. Just try to keep things in perspective – he is under a lot of stress and he may say and do things that are not typical of his character, or lash out at you for the simplest of things. Sometimes it's all part of getting married, other times it's the only way some of us can release that bundled up nervousness. In any case, if it does happen, be there for him, he'd do the same for you.

The pre-groom, groom

Your friend wasn't always the groom. In fact, up until moments ago, he was just some guy who was engaged to be married. I'm sure that you have been there for him since the beginning. It has been a long road leading up to this, his wedding day (unless of course he has made all of his decisions in haste, only knowing the bride-to-be hours before the actual wedding). In either case, you have probably had the opportunity to help him through many facets of the marrying ritual. Even the proposal, for example, has probably been practiced on you prior to him delivering it to his girlfriend. This is where caution and self-control may become a factor.

You can help him to avoid the pitfalls of the unsuccessful by reminding him what constitutes a reasonable proposal of marriage. Taste does speak for itself and sometimes the simplest forms of expression are the sincerest. However, even then, there can be the proposal from hell.

The Top Ten failed wedding proposals

10. Aw, C'mon.

9. As a matter of fact, I am the last man on earth.

8. I've changed since prison, really!
7. The only reason I'm asking you to be my wife is because you're pregnant.
6. Hey, the police couldn't make those bigamy charges stick.
5. You remind me of my mother.
4. I don't see the problem – Jerry Lee Lewis married his 13-year-old cousin.
3. You're the fourth girl I've asked this question of today.
2. Hey, how'd you like a green card?
1. It's the cheapest way I know of getting all new housewares.

So let's say that he does finally manage to get the appropriate words out and finds somebody to marry him. Then he will want you to be his best man. So what's next?

Sanity . . .

The general idea of the best man dates far before anyone can really remember. It has been suggested that the purpose of the best man is to act as a witness to the ceremony of marriage, but since anybody is capable of fulfilling this obligation, man or woman, why "best?" And although opinions differ in this regard, the real reason for the "best" man, in other words the very existence of one, is based on the character of the male gender itself.

As men we realize the need to have a friend, a partner or a colleague of the same sex (but not always), to administer sense to us when we feel that our own mind is not composed enough to do so on its own. This type of help is also sought when we have already made a decision on our own, and need the reassurances of others (or one "best" from the collective group) to confirm our thoughts.

We would never openly admit that we need somebody else's help. In fact, we often deny their participation. It is more that we want somebody to ensure that we do not go back on our words, and hold us to our self-promise.

Hence the role of the best man, to administer sanity to a man who seems to be losing his mind in the face of his approaching marriage.

Now I am not suggesting that when a man is about to get married, his mind turns to oatmeal and he cannot function as a human being without help. I am suggesting that the groom may be under a lot of duress or pressure, and might act in an irrational fashion because of this. Such is often not the case; however, there are some that feel that they have acted hastily in proposing, and often change their minds. Others feel trapped by their decision and just want a shoulder to lean on, or help in deciding their fate. Still others become emotional wrecks and require serious help.

How do we help them? Well, quite simply, be his friend. You're his friend, you will know the parameters of your friendship, and you should act appropriately within these confines to confront any issue that may trouble him.

Sanity exemplified
Kevin's and Susie's wedding

This story was submitted by a friend.

Whoever said that weddings were a hassle, I agree with them. That is, until my friend Kevin got married. Kevin and I have been friends forever, and when Kevin asked me to be his best man I was both thrilled and surprised. You see, Kevin has always been the sort of person that makes friends easily and keeps them all. This, combined with the fact that I would often go away for years at a time and we would lose touch with each other, was why I felt surprised that he picked me.

Kevin, on the other hand, liked to be part of his friends' lives always, often dividing his time equally among them. He always treated his friends (me included) as if it was he (Kevin) who was lucky to have us as a friend, when it was truly the other way around.

He had known Susie for several years. In fact, most of his close friends were also her close friends and vice versa, and a week before the wedding, Kevin confided in me that he was having second thoughts about getting married. I was shocked. It seems that he was worried that once he and Susie hitched up that he would have to spend all of his time at home with her, and soon his family, and lose track of his friends. At first I thought that he was joking, but this genuinely seemed to bother him.

I reasoned with him like any friend would, floored by his statement. I told him that things didn't have to change, even though, invariably they would because marriage has a way of getting the best of everyone, and for all of the right reasons.

I certainly didn't want to give Kevin an ultimatum, telling him that he had to choose between her and his friends. Although I knew that it was his decision, and he had to decide what was most important to him, I couldn't tell him this. I felt that if he picked his friends, I would have betrayed Susie, even though it wouldn't have been a selfish act on my part. I just wanted my friend to be equipped with all of the facts before making his final decision.

I told him that in life your friends you keep forever, and that if they are truly your friends, things do not come between you. I also told him that if Susie loved him (and I knew that she did), she would accept his lifestyle as being social (as she already did). I then told him that he shouldn't worry about what his friends might think if he didn't spend a lot of time with them, because a wife is more important and demands more time than a friend would. After all, I added, he doesn't have to go home every night and sleep with his friends. Susie can give him something far more important than any of his friends could ever hope to offer, and that she was his best friend, (as the song goes) a best friend with benefits. I just didn't want him to throw away Susie for the likes of me and I told him this.

"You and I will always be friends; sure we will fight, but in the end, we'll still be friends." I even reminded him that my not seeing him for several years hadn't harmed our friendship. "But, if you dump Susie, that's it. Sure, there might be a chance later, but there will always be the fact that you let her down once hanging over your heads. A certain lack of trust as it were. With friends you get over them and move on, learning to accept things, knowing never to do them again, or then again, maybe not."

He showed various reservations to my speech (or lecture), until I put it straight and told him that Susie was the best thing that ever happened to him, that if he blew this, most of his friends wouldn't want to be his friend anymore anyway, because he was so stupid. Ultimately though, if he truly wasn't happy with her, he really had to consider things and decide. "Besides," I added, "this may be the only chance I ever get to be somebody's best man."

That was when he caved in and told me the real reason he had cold feet. He confided in me why he always had a lot of friends and kept making new ones. It was because he was insecure that nobody liked him, and he went through life wanting to be liked, and went through great pains to do this. He also felt that he wasn't good enough for Susie. I laughed and reminded him that if this was truly the case, she wouldn't have agreed to spend the rest of her life with him by saying yes to his proposal of marriage. I also added that of all the people I had ever met, or had ever known about, that he was by far the most well-liked individual.

The wedding took place right on schedule, and to this very day we're all still very, very good friends.

Last chances . . .

If the groom manages to make it past stage two of the wedding test, and his sanity has remained intact, you are to provide a reminder to him of what his life was like before all of this ever happened. A last chance, as it were, to live it up before the "I do."

Yes, the bachelor party is considered the best man's foremost responsibility to the groom. Actually, if you stop to think about it, the bachelor party isn't so much a last chance celebration for the groom, but more a good-bye party thrown to him by his friends, to remove him from that elite society called bachelorhood. This opens up more room for the guys who are still single in which to work. We men are selfish that way, and hey, if there is an opportunity to drink in the company of entertaining professionals, we certainly don't need an excuse, no matter what the cause.

The rehearsal dinner

You didn't actually think that people got married without practicing first? Some people even get married several times before they get it right, and they still haven't perfected it to the point that something doesn't go wrong. But that's what life is all about, practicing. For what, I'm not quite sure.

Weddings, on the other hand, dictate, at least with those involved, that everything must be perfect. This is a very special day and they want to make it a very memorable occasion, and so to achieve this, they practice. Now don't worry, you won't have to give up your social life just because your friends are getting married, but you do have to practice with them. It's not like piano lessons. It's usually just a one-time deal, unless the rehearsal goes so badly that more practicing is required.

The rehearsal is usually required when the wedding ceremony is held at a hall/church, or when there are several participants involved, although many weddings have rehearsals anyway. The rehearsal or 'mock ceremony' is staged so that everybody is aware of the exact proceedings of the wedding ceremony, where to stand, how fast to walk, when to hand over the ring, etc.

Now that doesn't sound too complicated, does it? Well, you'd be surprised how many people forget much of what they practiced come wedding day, even after a rehearsal or two. Something happens between the rehearsal and the wedding. It's like a black hole in people's memories. And if this doesn't happen, something changes in the wedding ceremony itself to throw off everybody's timing. Hence the rehearsal, to be prepared for such circumstances.

The rehearsal also acts as a chance for everybody to get together. Seldom does everybody in the wedding party know each other, so the rehearsal allows you to meet, greet and talk with your fellow wedding party members.

The best man is usually the emcee at the rehearsal dinner. For the most part, since this is a very casual affair, a simple get-together, no major preparation is usually required. However, the best man does prepare and offer a speech about the bride and groom. The length and content of this speech varies, and is usually delivered with humor, as the people in attendance are few and generally quite close.

If you do feel the need to offer a more adequately prepared speech for the occasion, perhaps because you will not have this responsibility at the wedding itself, you may refer to the chapter on speeches, and simply alter any of them to make it more appropriate for this smaller venue.

Aside from speaking at this engagement, the other primary focus should be to enjoy yourself, and if you have the honor of further orations at the wedding, this dinner can also provide a wealth of material for a speech you may have to give at the reception.

You will probably have to give the toast to the bridesmaids at the wedding reception. This can be difficult, in particular if you don't know them. So you can extract as much information as possible at the rehearsal, or at the rehearsal dinner, to properly write a decent speech.

The other speech that you may be required to give at the wedding is the first toast to the bride and groom, and its contents should be reflective of those in attendance at the wedding.

In the event that you do not know what to say in your toast, or if you feel that you do not have enough material, this rehearsal dinner can certainly be a great place to get some. Of course, you probably won't need too much information about the groom, but relating how excited, nervous or insane he has been prior to the wedding, or at this dinner, is always a nice touch. The same goes for the bride, talk to her friends, watch her and record everything. Then later, simply sort through the events that have transpired, things that you have learned and information that you've collected, until you have what you want to say.

Having got the groom this far, and managing to both learn something in the process, you are well on your way in becoming a first rate best man. This, however, was the easy part, and the wedding itself is the real test.

Getting the groom to the church on time.

It's really quite funny when you think about it. I mean, he is a grown man and he shouldn't need anybody's, let alone your, help to get to the church on time for his own wedding. But you would be surprised how many grooms have faltered in this regard, much to the chagrin of their bride-to-be, waiting in front of all those people.

So how do you get the groom dressed and ready for his big day without any major incident? There are some obvious answers, but for those extra special circumstances, I have included a few more for your reference.

☞ Keep reminding him that the wedding actually starts earlier than he thinks.

☞ Change all of the clocks in his house ahead one-hour, or if you live in a very small town, get everybody involved.

☞ Tell him that all of the guys are going to get together at the church early to play a few rounds of poker before the wedding starts.

☞ Tell him that they are having an early bird draw.

☞ The sooner the wedding is over, the sooner the reception starts.

☞ Remind him that it's later someplace else in the world right now.

☞ Sleep at the church the night before the wedding.

☞ Since you may actually be the one that is always late and not the groom, have somebody do all of these things for you!

That extra mile . . .

A perfect example of going that extra mile in the time of crisis is related in the following pages, just so you can get an idea of how easily things can go astray. With the help of a well-placed best man, and a little compromise, things can get back on track. A friend contributed this piece.

Brian and Mike were best friends for many years and it was no surprise when Brian asked Mike to be his best man at his wedding. Brian had been known as the type of person who always did things at the last minute – he liked to call it "being a fourth quarter player" – and why should his wedding be any different. Naturally the bride-to-be, Sandra, was already well aware of what she was getting into, having dated Brian for two years prior to the big day, and she prepared herself well for any mishap that might have ensued due to "Brian's way."

So far things had seemed to be going well. Mike was what you would call somewhat meticulous, speaking euphemistically, and he and Brian always made a good team, their behavior often off-setting each others' like a modern-day odd couple.

Mike kept Brian running on schedule with minor setbacks as expected. They were only 15 minutes late for the rehearsal, and Brian was fully dressed. This was a miracle by most standards.

When the wedding day arrived, Brian told Mike that the tuxedo they had rented and picked up over a week ago had managed to get its pants zipper broken one night when Brian was trying them on.

Mikes first response was to question Brian's timing, but as history certainly dictated, Brian's answer was invariably "What's the rush?

We'll just pick them up on the way." On their way to the wedding, the groom wore sweat pants with his tuxedo jacket into a store to buy a new pair of pants.

The clerk was helpful in every detail, except in how to hem Brian's pants for him in 10 minutes. Mike jumped in and borrowed the stapler from the counter and proceeded to staple a hemline into the bottom of Brian's pants. They were off.

At the wedding, to which they showed up right on time, Mike noticed that Brian, while putting on his pants, was wearing white sport socks complete with the brand name logo on them. When asked where his black socks were, Brian simply replied that he had forgotten to take them when he grabbed his shoes. Mike was at least grateful that he had remembered his shoes, or else he would have been married in running shoes. This wasn't good enough for Mike, so he took a black marker and proceeded to color in the area of Brian's socks that showed up as best as he could under the circumstances (as they were pressed for time).

The wedding went off without a hitch, and nobody made mention of the staple line in Brian's pants. There were, however, several comments about Brian's socks when he sat down in the church to sign the register, and his pant legs rode up his calf exposing his two-tone sport socks to all those in attendance.

Everyone seemed pleased that this was the only thing that they noticed, thanks to the best man Mike.

Chapter Four
The Bride

It certainly wouldn't be a wedding without both the groom and the bride. "Oh yeah, the bride, isn't she the one in the white dress? So you mean I'm responsible for her too? What about the bridesmaid? Why do I have to pull this double duty?"

You were more than likely chosen to be the best man by the groom. However, I'm quite sure that your position was discussed by both parties, making you, in fact, "their" best man. I'm sure that many a wedding has ended in disaster because of the groom's choice of his second, the bride having differences with him. In consideration of this, you are required, as much or as little as you like, to be responsible to the bride as well.

For the most part, you are probably already quite close to the lady, having known her through your friend, the groom, or through various other sources. A bond or friendship with the bride strengthens your ability to become a first rate best man. From her standpoint, you possess information that is vital to her well being, because you can talk her husband-to-be through some selfish deliberations (should I . . . shouldn't I . . . get up on stage and dance with that girl?). You will want her to convey her trust in you (particularly where the bachelor party is concerned, or you may never get to see your friend again).

Responsibilities to the bride vary somewhat depending on your relationship with her. It is rare that she would ask something of you if she did not know you, but that doesn't mean that you can't offer your services. After all, you will probably see a lot of her when you visit your friend.

When the bride does request something from you, it is, in one way or another, related to her husband-to-be. These types of requests usually come when you are about to take her man out on his night of bachelor party fun. Women are not blind to what these parties usually entail, even with our insistence that there will be nothing seedy or demeaning in any of the activities involved. We, of course, are lying through our teeth, but it's okay, they know that.

Brides are often less concerned with the particulars of the party, than with what we have in store for their husbands. They trust their men to go out and have fun – if they didn't he wouldn't be going. Who they don't trust is you and your friends.

Now I'm not saying that she regards you with contempt for trying to corrupt her husband-to-be. On the contrary, she is merely looking out for the best interests of her man. What could be the harm in that?

Simply put, there are guidelines that we must follow in order to appease the bridal mind. We usually agree to anything that they suggest, or order in some cases, shrugging it off later.

They offer these suggestions, or subtle threats to our genitals, knowing full well that we will ignore most of them, and this is when they try to convince their husbands not to be taken in by the guile of life-long friends.

She in turn is often reassured by his convincing tones, not fully aware that in a few short hours he will be spineless and have no control whatsoever over the 30 or so people that he regards as friends. These same friends seek to destroy the very fabric of his moral side, casting him into drunken ridicule. But that's what friends are for.

The careful best man will try to avoid situations that may cause a rift in future relations. Keep in mind that what you abuse at these early stages will be carried over to many weekends in the future. Your seemingly harmless fishing trip will be unveiled for what it really is, a drunken guy weekend, and your friend will not be able to attend because of what you did to him at his bachelor party.

There are several ways around this type of behavior. The simplest of all is to abide by her wishes. This does not mean that there is no room for compromise. A few simple ground rules are usually accepted, and they really have no bearing on the rest of the evening.

Requests from the Bride

Many requests given by the bride-to-be regarding bachelor parties are as follows:

Her Request:	I want him to look the same as when I dropped him off.
Your Compromise:	Any skin or body parts hidden by clothes are fair game.
Her Request:	Leave all hair from the neck up.
Your Compromise:	Allow ample time for re-growth. In other words, try to schedule the bachelor party three weeks before the wedding so that you are free to do as you please. A wedding scheduled a few days after the party is often delayed because of these re-growth periods.
Her Request:	Don't do anything to him that will be permanent. In other words, no tattoos.
Your Compromise:	Emotional scarring is okay.
Her Request:	I don't want him to get too drunk.
Your Compromise:	It will take him three days to sober up instead of the usual five.
Her Request:	No nudity.
Your Compromise:	I promise to keep all of his clothes on.
Her Request:	Don't keep him out too late, he has to work in the morning
Your Compromise:	It's okay – I've invited his boss along too.
Her Request:	He had better not come home drunk, he can't afford to miss another day at work.
Your Compromise:	He's talented, it won't take him long to find another job.
Her Request:	There had better not be any hookers at the party.
Your Compromise:	Meet the hookers in the parking lot.

Her Request:	I want him to be okay when I pick him up after the party.
Your Compromise:	By the time he figures out that we got him drunk and put him on the plane to Bora-Bora, you won't have any problem at the airport.
Her Request:	Nothing dirty.
Your Compromise:	Don't worry, he'll be wearing an over-sized condom on his head all night.
Her Request:	I don't want any women to be jumping out of a cake.
Your Compromise:	We'll have them wrestle in Jell-O instead.
Her Request:	I hope you don't mind my father going along to chaperone.
Your Compromise:	I hope your mother doesn't mind your father dancing with $100/hr strippers.
Her Request:	I don't want you guys doing anything that demoralizes women.
Your Compromise:	Demoralizing your husband is okay then.
Her Request:	I don't want him doing anything he'll regret later.
Your Compromise:	We promise not to convince him to marry anyone else.
Her Request:	I don't want him tempted in any way.
Your Compromise:	That's okay, I hear the church is very forgiving.
Her Request:	The last time he went to a bachelor party, he was sick for three days.
Your Compromise:	You are right, three days isn't long enough. Let's go for the record.
Her Request:	If he comes home in a mess he had better not expect me to take care of him.
Your Compromise:	Don't worry, that's what the people at the de-tox clinic get paid for.
Her Request:	You better not bring him home drunk, throwing up on all the carpets.
Your Compromise:	Don't worry, he'll have had his stomach pumped long before that.
Her Request:	Please don't do anything that will ruin my wedding.

Your Compromise: Please refrain from watching the television or reading the newspapers for three days after the party.

Her Request: No tattoos.

Your Compromise: Bring on the body piercing.

Her Request: No drugs.

Your Compromise: Tell him that in the morning when he's begging you for some aspirin.

Her Request: Don't do anything illegal.

Your Compromise: Extradition can often take many years.

Her Request: Try to have fun.

Your Compromise: We will.

Personal requests . . .

On more than one occasion, the lovely bride-to-be has requested that I return her man the same way she dropped him off, and this story pretty well sums up how I usually handle these situations.

My friend Marty was best man for Dale and Carla's wedding, some friends of ours, and of course a bachelor party was arranged. Since I had experience in this field, Marty asked me to help out. My official responsibility, apart from advice, was to get the groom drunk. Carla had trust in Marty, but knew that once I was involved, things could get ugly, so she specifically approached me and asked (more like warned) me to return her man the way she dropped him off. I thought about her request and agreed, knowing full well that her words were so extremely vague that I had plenty of room to work and plenty of excuses if the shit hit the proverbial fan.

The night got underway with everybody meeting at Marty's apartment, that way we could all catch cabs and not have to worry about driving, and then heading to the restaurant for the festivities. Luckily Marty phoned ahead to reconfirm our reservation, because the restaurant had a power failure, and was considering closing unless power was restored.

In the meantime we just sat around and waited. Since Marty was not prepared for guests, he was lacking in the usual refreshments of choice, except for a few ounces from several bottles and a scant variety of bottled beer and coolers. This was certainly not enough to please this rowdy group. I immediately insisted that these resources should be given to the groom, and everybody heartily agreed.

The boys kept busy playing cards while I prepared several concoctions from the various hodge-podge of liquors available. Most of them were made into shooters and administered to the groom at various intervals.

I had almost exhausted my supply of beverages, and the restaurant had still not called, so I improvised. What was once strictly straight alcohol, was now diluted with beer and wine coolers. This soon progressed to drops of the hard stuff, with drops of beer, grenadine and dish soap. It sounds terrible, but I assure you it had a rather soothing effect on the groom, not to mention that it slowed down the intoxication process with all of the dilution.

Needless to say, the groom had a sufficient glow about him, so I proceeded with my next phase of fun. Remembering Carla's concerns, I took out a black magic marker and prompted the bachelor attendees to write something of note on our groom, reminding them that we had to return him the same as when he was dropped off. Dale was quickly relieved of his shirt, and we proceeded to draw over this entire area of his body, but only up to his neck and wrist lines (so that it would not be visible when he had his shirt on, thus keeping my promise to Carla – sort of). I took the choice spot, the navel, and I must admit, he had a pretty deep belly button. Apparently it took both Dale and Carla weeks to finally get his navel totally clean.

The restaurant finally phoned, and dinner was cancelled, so we quickly made other arrangements, and the troops rallied to make this evening work. While someone ran out for beverages, Marty called the stripper that was supposed to meet us at the restaurant and asked her to dance at his place. This increased her fee, but we didn't mind. The evening progressed with pizza, beer and a professional woman dancing on Marty's coffee table, a good night in most respects.

Later we headed to the local watering hole, where I resumed my duties as alcohol coordinator, and started to order shooters non-stop. The groom insisted, based on my other recipes I'm sure, that I join him in every shot. This I had no problem with, however, the waitress seemed a little miffed when I kept throwing my shot over my shoulder onto the floor. The groom was never the wiser, and even remarked on my stoic ability to handle my liquor.

Soon Dale was, well, hammered, drunk, blasted, wasted (pick one) and he felt that his safest place was the men's room. Everybody else was enjoying themselves and didn't notice that Dale had not returned after half an hour. Most of us just assumed that he was hugging the porcelain. Finally, Marty and I went in to investigate. There was poor Dale sitting on the bathroom floor, glad to see his friends again. He began to hug us, and insisted that we take him out of there.

The bathroom was painted in the most hideous color scheme. It was orange and purple and green. After getting sick, Dale thought he was imagining these colors, thinking he was in bachelor party hell. To further add to his confusion, the back of the bathroom door had a sign on it that read "women." (Many bars do this, on the back of the ladies room door it says men, telling us that this door leads us back to our dates). Dale, who was very drunk and confused in this nightmare of a bathroom, thought that his only escape was through the ladies room. He desperately looked for another door, or secret panel, only to find nothing. He was far too shy to burst into the ladies room, or so he thought it was, to escape, so he just sat there waiting for help.

Carla arrived shortly afterwards to pick up her husband-to-be, Dale having called her prior to his bathroom adventure, and she seemed rather irate, particularly at me. I was only thankful that I was not at their house when she helped Dale undress for bed.

Request fulfilled . . .

There are other occasions, however, when the best man rises to his position and genuinely helps the bride. This is actually the norm for most weddings, and the story above certainly didn't cause any rifts in relations, rather, it just brought a little mistrust into the situation.

The best man should be prepared for all types of scenarios. Nothing is ever certain, especially when it comes to a wedding, or worse, a group of men embarking on a bachelor party. A lot of things can go wrong and often do. How does that saying go, something about the best-laid plans? What about barely-laid plans? Which is how most bachelor parties are put together. Consider that these are men we are talking about and that for the most part we have a plan, or rather an outline of a plan, and the ability or desire to just let things progress on their own. Mob rules, group mentality, call it what you want, but you are always hard pressed to drag a bunch of half drunk (or is it half sober) individuals around town without hesitation, confusion and conflict. This can lead you down several roads that you were not prepared to travel.

I may be assuming the worst, and when you are in the middle of it, it never really seems as bad as it is. In fact, it is usually quite fun, and even memorable. However, something makes a lot of these circumstances unbearable – the repercussions. (What a terrible word). Why does everything we do have to have an effect on everything else that we do? If I had the answer, I wouldn't need to write for a living. But it does, and in this we must consider the bride in particular.

That extra mile . . .

The best man's relationship to the bride does not always revolve around the bachelor party. In fact, sometimes it is never even a factor. Often it is the little things that we do that get noticed, the thank-you that is left unsaid, but understood, or the true-to-form sacrifices that truly make us best men.

A perfect example of going the distance is as follows.

Holy shiner Batman

Mike and Linda wanted to have their wedding at a large ski resort, and get married on the slopes. Obviously, decorations were pretty much provided by nature, a soft snowy mountain, green trees to witness the event, and the entire world below them, beneath the clouds.

The best man Peter had a number of responsibilities in this regard, since he lived in the area and Mike and Linda did not. The wedding party was small and not very formal, as weather dictated. This snowy locale didn't permit such luxuries as the tuxedo, unless it was down filled. Matching outfits was also an extreme reach, but the color chosen by the individuals in attendance was suitable.

Peter had a considerable time trying to find a minister to perform the ceremony. First, they needed one who would offer his services on a mountaintop covered in snow and second, who would do all of this while on skis. This was a difficult task because the ceremony required that skis be worn to access the chosen site, although some guests opted to trudge their way down the slope to the altar, only to trudge their way back up, while the rest of those in attendance swished their way down the slopes.

The day before the wedding, Peter proved his worthiness. Relaxing in the chalet after a couple of runs, Peter, Gord (a friend of the couple's) and the bride Linda returned to the slopes for what was to be a wonderful afternoon of skiing. When they got to the ski rack where everybody had left their things, Linda's ski poles were gone. Peter noticed a couple of fellows trying to make a hasty exit and confronted them about the similarities in their ski poles and Lea's missing pair.

Denial was offered rather than excuse, so Peter asked again, except this time not so polite. The accused got agitated and, with Peter's continued insistence, broke down and punched Peter in the face above his eye, dropped the ski poles and fled down the hill.

Later that day, again relaxing in the chalet, we were discussing what had happened earlier when somebody noticed Peter's face. It seems that with the temperature change between indoors and out, the man's punch was visible on Peter's face. Upon closer inspection, three knuckle marks could be clearly seen on his forehead just above his left eye. At this point Gord piped in, "Peter I can count one, two, three knuckle marks on your forehead, what happened to the fourth one?" To which Peter promptly replied, "Well, I like to think I dodged one."

The next day during the ceremony, Peter's face showed no sign of the previous day's events, the cold weather masking his entire face in a red wintry glow. Linda was able to use her ski poles for support during the ceremony, and the wedding was a wonderful success thanks to the knight in the shining Gortex.

The lovely bride-to-be, the symbol of happiness to your friend, a symbol of his love everlasting, a woman who, if you don't take care of her, may never allow your friend to talk to you again. But if you can manage to get the groom on track, his bride-to-be surely cannot be any more of a challenge. Besides, the wedding is the big thing.

Chapter Five
Wedding Preparations

It can sometimes be said that weddings are difficult things to organize, especially if you have no idea what you are doing. This is usually the case because most of us aren't married so often that we can consider ourselves professionals. So we must rely on the expertise of those who have been married before us, and those before them, handed down through the generations until it is finally your turn to live through disaster. Still, there are those who may be considered professionals. For some of us (the deranged organizers, intent on doing everything ourselves) this has become a life's work, and some people make a considerable amount of money doing so. To these hard working souls I both salute and condemn you. People like you make it all the more difficult for us regular folk to organize a decent wedding without the comparison of one of your fantastically ornate affairs being thrown in our faces. Thank goodness that, for the most part, the best man is usually exempt from such trifles.

In the organizing department, the best man's responsibility can best be described as pitching in, lending a hand or making oneself scarce. It really depends on the individuals getting married, asking for the help of their closest peers, and the individual offering to help his lovesick friends.

Weddings nowadays can be a little more complex compared to the affairs of the past, and it is because of this that the role of the best man has increased throughout the years.

Traditional weddings, for the most part (those involving a church for example, or religious ceremony of some sort), have remained exactly that, traditional, except for the fact that everybody wants their wedding to be somewhat different from everybody else's. They still want a traditional wedding, but they bend it at the sides until it takes on a unique shape, thereby making it special. In order to accomplish this, something gets slightly changed (they write their own vows, they change the location, animals are brought in, etc.) or an effect is added (poems, songs, circus clowns) to enhance the ceremony into an individual affair.

Naturally, many of these changes involve supervision or help in order to carry them out, to see them through to fruition so to speak, and since the best man, in most eyes, has the fewest responsibilities, this job is usually heaped onto his plate.

Oh, don't be fooled by those who claim that they want to have a simple wedding, void of anything too fancy, and start to think that this will be very easy for you, because you won't have added responsibilities. Translated, this usually means that they want to have an extremely elaborate affair, but they don't want to pay the big bucks to have it. This is where you come in. You see, under normal conditions, weddings carry on under the pretense that money is not worth worrying about, and that if you like the looks of something, or that it matches the color scheme, or theme, of the wedding, you buy it without worrying about the cost. This is not to say that people become frivolous, haphazardly throwing away their money on something just because it is pink, but rather that money becomes a secondary concern.

When money is a factor, however, all of the above still applies, except now, rather than buying those pink flowers just because of the color, you are to find the very best price for attaining this effect (different types of flowers that are less expensive, white flowers with pink mixed in or white flowers dyed to look pink . . .). The bottom line is that this usually creates a lot of shopping around, and since there are a lot of factors that contribute to the organization of a wedding, you are often required to help out in some way or another.

If you are lucky, you may only have to be the driver or errand boy. Although I have been the telephone inquiries guy a few times and that is not so bad either. You call several places (florists, reception halls, caterers, etc.), getting different quotes on what they offer. The bride, et al., usually give you parameters of what they want, and you simply dial and ask, dial and ask. This is pretty monotonous stuff, but it was easy so I never complained.

Aside from these simple services that you can render, there are several others left to do. In one wedding of which I was a part, the family and friends essentially did everything by themselves, and I might add the outcome was fantastic.

In this wedding almost everything was done by hand. Many of the flowers for the centerpieces came from the gardens of family and friends, and were arranged by an aunt who had a flair for that sort of thing. All of the decorations at the hall were prepared by some of ladies of the neighborhood. Even all of the food was made ahead of time, stored, brought and served at the wedding reception. During the reception, some of these eccentric cooks even got up to the microphone and announced that there was still a lot a food that needed to be eaten, and that nobody was going to leave until it was all finished. Hey, this type of helping out, I didn't mind.

This wedding was an exception I am sure, but there still remains the obvious fact that weddings can be difficult to put together. There is organizing, collecting, making, preparing, booking, registering, ordering, checking, searching, licensing, testing, renting, signing, feeding, eating, paying, reserving, hoping, wishing and a list far too detailed to bother continuing. As for these requirements and complex settings, fear not, because organized heads will prevail, and you will be instructed, if needed at all, as to what you will be required to do.

Suffice it to say that the wedding may dictate any number of responsibilities, and that you may be asked to help out in regards to any one of these variables. If you are very lucky though, the couple will decide to get married at city hall, or better yet, to elope.

I just wanted the reader to be aware of the complexity of today's so called traditional weddings, and I haven't even touched on the alternative weddings yet, and thankfully, I won't, since we are more concerned with the wedding as a ceremony and not as an institution.

The main purpose . . .

The main purpose of the best man at the wedding is to act as a witness to the ceremony, and to sign the wedding register stating exactly that. Marriage is a legal contract/obligation between two people, in the eyes of God or in the eyes of the government (state), and therefore witnesses are necessary to prove that this union did in fact take place. All of the other things that a best man is involved in are secondary. This reasoning makes the wedding seem more like a business merger than a happy event, and so over the years people have created this elaborate affair (the wedding ceremony) to make one's marriage a more personal thing. Gladly, it has worked.

Other duties that lead the best man and the happy couple to this day have already been discussed, however, the best man does, or may have, a few important roles to play at the wedding ceremony.

Other than to act as a witness, the best man is often responsible for holding the wedding ring for the groom (more on that in the next chapter).

Another responsibility of the best man, as well as the other groomsmen (or ushers as they are sometimes called), is to seat the arriving guests prior to the ceremony (friends of the bride's side, or friends of the groom's side). Usually, the best man is not required to perform this task, as he is usually still en route with the groom, and doesn't arrive until long after all of the guests have grown impatient. However, when the best man is responsible enough to show up on time, he can certainly lend a hand in this department.

One final responsibility, and a responsibility not widely known I might add, is to act as the wedding bouncer. Your job here is to turf any ex-boyfriends who get it inside their heads that the happy bride still has a thing for them. They decide to crash the wedding by objecting when the priest, etc., offers the opportunity, thereby ruining your friend's life and your chances of a free meal at the reception.

If this should ever happen, don't worry about discretion, since this person obviously didn't. Even if it is Dustin Hoffman (remember *The Graduate*?), send his sorry butt flying.

Okay, now that we know what the best man is supposed to do, let's recap the wedding ceremony. Get the groom to the ceremony on time, seat people, stand next to the groom (remember not to object), give him the ring, sign the register (wedding certificate), look happy. There, it seems simple enough doesn't it? Of course it always doesn't go this well.

Wedding mishaps

We've all been to weddings where something, even a little thing, goes wrong. In fact, most of us could say that we have never been to a perfect wedding. I know that I haven't. So why fret, let it happen and get on with the rest of the festivities. There is always that very first wedding to be perfect. I'm sure you would even have your names bronzed or something to commemorate such an occasion, being held in such high esteem for accomplishing something that nobody else has ever achieved.

Now I am exaggerating. I'm quite sure that many a wedding has gone off without a hitch. What I am saying is that with so much to prepare and ready, sometimes small things get overlooked, or sudden surprises pop up out of nowhere. These should all be taken in stride, although usually one or more people may assume the burden of the stress and anxiety of it all. These people we thank, one, for taking the responsibility away from us; two, for not flipping out too much about the whole thing . . . then again.

Here are some examples of instances where things get out of hand, and what effect it had on everybody, if any, at the wedding. This first two were sent in by friends.

Mistaken identity

John and Sandy had a traditional Catholic Church wedding. When they were standing at the altar being married, the priest introduced the couple to those in attendance. "We are here today to witness the joining of these two souls, Sandy and Steve, in holy matrimony." Sandy thought this was pretty funny and turned to Steve, John's brother, who was sitting in the front row, and said "Hey, Steve you better get up here, I guess I'm supposed to marry you today and not

John." *Everybody laughed, including Steve who couldn't stop, and he laughed so hard that he broke the buttons on his shirt.*

Needless to say, the priest apologized for his error, adding that John looked so much like Steve that he made a mistake.

The organizer from hell

This wedding had all the makings of disaster right from the start, or so Helen, Sarah's mother, thought. Helen was adamant that nobody could properly plan and execute the wedding unless it was her doing it, so she did everything. She wanted her daughter's wedding to be perfect, although some say that it possessed her and it no longer became Sarah's wedding but Helen's wedding.

As things progressed, Sarah had to admit that her mother's intervention seemed to pay off, because things ran very smoothly. The wedding itself took place at a ski lodge, but during the summer time. That way they could take full advantage of the wonderful scenery, but without the expense of the weather.

It was a wonderful morning wedding, and in the afternoon several guests gathered to try their luck at driving a golf ball up the slopes, trying to hit the chair lift poles. Everybody who played put money into a pot, and whoever hit the farthest pole got the pot; if nobody succeeded in winning, the bride and groom would get the money to use on their honeymoon. Of course nobody won, not so much for the lack of effort, but more so for the level of intoxication.

This carried over until dinner in the late afternoon and several guests were a little rambunctious, but far from out of line. During a replay of the afternoon, one of the guests, emulating his golf-swing, knocked over a tray of fruit. This seemed to go unnoticed except for "Helen the organizer," who was fully aware of what had happened. She immediately flew over to the guest and reamed him out for his behavior. Several guests tried to calm her down, offering apologetic words, but were promptly dismissed for being bad influences on her daughter, and only causing trouble out of jealousy of a perfect wedding. An argument then ensued, and Helen, at the end of her stress cord, flipped out and demanded that everybody leave.

A story about cake

Every wedding has a story and every wedding has a cake, so now it is time to tell a story about a wedding cake.

Now this story isn't your typical wedding cake story. We all know that there are certainly enough wedding cake stories floating around, and we don't need to have to sit through another one. But this one, a wedding I actually attended, is different. Read on and you'll understand what I am saying.

John and Jessica had one dream, to have a wonderful life together. They had, up until John's proposal, a happy life living together, but Jessica wanted more, and John's proposal brought with it even more happiness and joy than Jessica ever thought possible. This was a chance for her dream life to come true.

John and Jessica were simple people with simple goals. They never liked to clutter their lives with difficulties they could not handle, and so when it came to their wedding, they wanted a simple affair with a few friends.

Jessica had hand made her own dress, because she thought that spending all that money on a dress that she was going to wear once was a waste, and they had better things they could use the money on. She even insisted to John, having discussed it many times with him, that when he finally proposed that it wasn't necessary for him to spend a lot of money on a ring. She felt that the act of him proposing, wanting to spend the rest of his life with her, was more of a symbol than any ring could offer. The ring that John offered to her was simple and elegant and she wore it with grace, proudly on her finger.

The wedding was also to be a simple affair. They wanted to have the ceremony performed in an old country church. A small one-roomed church with a steeple would be the backdrop to the start of their new lives together. There, in the presence of God and a few close friends and relatives, would they be united in holy matrimony.

The reception would also be a simple gathering. A nice meal, some music and dancing. Jessica and John wanted to capture the closeness that one feels at Christmas or Thanksgiving throughout their wedding. The food was to be simply prepared and served with delicious, but inexpensive, wine. Even the cake was to be simple, perhaps one baked by her aunt, who always made a delicious one.

Their parents were very respecting of their wishes, and left them alone to their own planning of their wedding, offering help when needed or asked. The parents did, however, make one suggestion, and that was to let them supply the wedding cake. This was a difficult request, because both sets of parents wanted to supply the cake, suggesting that their cake would be the most extravagant. At first John and Jessica refused, knowing full well the situation would escalate, but with a little prodding and the persistent stubbornness of their parents, they agreed to let both sets of parents collaborate on the cake.

Jessica and John continued to live their lives in happiness, awaiting the day when they could become complete. Little did they know of the trouble brewing in the background. It seems that there was some argument between the parents as to the shape of the cake, and when that was resolved, the number of tiers was argued over. In fact no detail of the cake could be agreed upon. When responding to John and Jessica's questions regarding the delay, they simply offered that a cake so detailed, such as this, took time to create, and could not just be made. John and Jessica waited patiently, giving their parents the chance to help.

The bakers involved in the cake process, as there were several, were quite irate with all of the criticism of their work, and most of them quit. The Baker, or rather architect, who finally agreed to design the cake, made several different designs before his sixth was finally accepted by the reluctant parents, both insisting that it still was not perfect.

The cake itself was truly beautiful. The baker painstakingly put his soul into the work, and the result was nothing less than spectacular. So much so in fact that the cake caught the eye of magazine that wanted to do an article on the baker and his wonderful creation. The parents were simply tickled pink with the knowledge that their work-of-art was to be on display for the world to see. The only problem was that the article could not be done until after the wedding. The magazine did offer to send some photographers to the wedding along with the baker, to take pictures of the fabulous cake, and the parents were even more elated.

John and Jessica had a difficult time trying to accept this entire fanfare, particularly when their parents wanted to change the site of the reception. A cozy quaint family bistro owned by a friend of the couple became a larger venue with better lighting to accommodate the photography and grandeur of the cake. Certainly one could not have such a spectacular cake at such a simple affair, and so the parents began to rearrange the wedding. The main focus of the wedding soon became the cake, and not John and Jessica, but like the simple people they were, they went along with their parents' wishes, or so their parents thought.

When the wedding day finally arrived, John and Jessica didn't show up at that big church where their parents had decided the wedding would be. Nor did they show up at the big hall, where their reception was to be held. John and Jessica, with a select few of their friends in attendance, were married that morning in a quaint little one-roomed country church in front of God.

Later, they retired to a little bistro for dinner. There they enjoyed simple fare with their guests. They shared this moment, the happiest day of their life, drinking, dancing, laughing and loving, all in the absence of any cake. In fact, it was even requested by the couple that the word cake not even be mentioned, and all in attendance had fruit for dessert.

These next two incidents were told to me by friends.

Candid photos

The only mishap at this particular wedding was when Tony, insisting that he had to go to the bathroom just after the ceremony, did so. Unfortunately his zipper broke as he was trying to do up his pants. The unfortunate part of this story is that they were on their way to have their pictures taken when this happened. The professional pictures were not a problem as the photographer could edit out the areas that were exposed. However, the family and friend pictures left too much open for Tony's liking, so his best man Aldo insisted that all of the wedding pictures be taken with the men in the wedding party standing sideways. The other option was that they all undo their zippers so that the groom didn't look the fool in all of the pictures. Most opted for the side shots.

Slap, slap, I love you

There is an interesting story about a couple who lived together for many years prior to getting married. The groom-to-be was obviously afraid of commitment on such a level and often shrugged off the woman's attempts to discuss marriage. Finally he succumbed and the happy date was set.

As it happens, the night before the blessed event, the couple, not much for the tradition of being separated before the wedding, slept together in their bed as usual. During the night, the groom was riddled with strange dreams, none of which he would repeat, except to his best man, and he struggled in his sleep. He soon roused from his sleep to find that in his struggling, he had accidentally elbowed his bride-to-be in the face just below her eye. Having been awakened because of the sharp pain, the poor woman looked for the source of her discomfort, and found her husband-to-be tormented in sleep.

The next day, the wedding day, her face was extremely swollen and she had a black eye. She covered her face as best she could with make-up, but it was no use, there was no way to hide the swelling. They contemplated postponing the wedding, but the bride was reluctant to let anything delay something she had waited so long to fulfill. This is when the best man stepped in. Aware of the tormenting dreams and their unfortunate outcome, he proposed a plan that would hopefully take all of the focus off of the bride's face. After all, the bride is supposed to be the center of attention, usually as the most beautiful woman in the room and not the most hideously deformed, so everybody in the wedding party spent the day with make-up on their faces to resemble the bride's. Everybody at first thought it was planned, but word did get out of what had really happened and the best man was thanked for his quick, although unusual suggestion.

Needless to say the photographs were taken a week later, although some people did manage to get a few interesting photographs of the blessed event.

If men were in charge of weddings

A friend of mine submitted this to me, and although I think it is somewhat sexist, I have included it anyway.

1. There would be a Rehearsal Dinner Toga Party.
2. Bridesmaids would wear matching bikini tops and cut-off blue jeans.
3. Instead of tuxedos, all the guys would wear matching bowling shirts and running shoes with matching team colors.
4. June weddings would be scheduled around basketball play-offs.
5. Vows would mention cooking and sex specifically, but omit that "forsaking all others" part.
6. The couple would leave the ceremony in a souped up '73 Charger or some other hot rod with racing tires and flame designs on the side of the car. Better yet, a Harley!
7. Idiots who tried to dance with the bride (unless they were really old) would get punched in the head.
8. Big, slobbery dogs would be eligible for the role of "Best Man."
9. There would be "Tailgate Receptions."
10. Outdoor weddings would be held during sporting events at half time, or between innings.
11. Ceremonies would be short and honeymoons would be long.
12. Ceremonies and honeymoons would be inexpensive compared to the cost of the bachelor party. Those strippers and liquor sure do add up.

13. Men wouldn't ask, "Well, what do you think, dear? The burgundy or the wine colored napkins?" They'd just grab extras from their local pub or tavern.
14. Favors would be matchbooks and cigars. Better yet, free drink passes at the local lounge.
15. The bride's dress would show cleavage, her navel and be form-fitted to her rear.
16. Instead of a sit-down dinner or a buffet, there would be a hog roast or buckets of chicken, pizza and plenty of barbeque.
17. No one would bother with that "Veil Routine." But they would insist that the garter be as high up on her leg as it could go.
18. The bridal bouquet would be recycled from a previous funeral or something.
19. Invitations would read as follows . . . Tom (Dick or Harry) is getting the old ball and chain . . . He's getting married. He either:

    A) Knocked her up

    B) Couldn't get a different roommate

    C) Caved in to her ultimatum.

    Please meet the woman who will cook and clean for him for the rest of his life at Soldier Field Stadium, on the 50-Yard Line, at half-time during Sunday's Game.

Now that the wedding ceremony is over, you think it's time for you to kick back and relax, and why not? You've certainly earned it, haven't you? Well, for the most part, you are right, the serious part is over, the ceremony. They are officially married now and there isn't anything that can change that fact. You didn't even screw up or anything, but there is time for that at the reception.

Chapter Six
The Ring

The long-standing tradition of having the best man hold the ring has a number of stories behind its admission as part of the official ceremony; we'll list some here for you.

It is said that the groom bestows this privilege on the best man to keep the groom from having second thoughts and returning the ring, using the money to skip town. Of course, there is nothing to stop the best man from doing this also.

It has also been said that with all of the planning involved in organizing the wedding, and all of the stress that the groom is under, just getting himself to the church on time is enough responsibility. Therefore a second party is brought in to help him out with both, and since you need a witness anyway . . . dump these responsibilities on him.

Further stories suggest that if the groom should lose the ring, the symbol of his eternal love, it is considered bad luck (obviously); so entrusting it to somebody else to lose takes the heat off of the groom.

Since the best man is merely a witness, and to fully justify his presence at the ceremony, the tradition of ring holder holds more significance (and less legal ramification) over merely being the witness. Hence the introduction of the maid of honor as secondary witness, and to round out the equality of the wedding party.

A less likely reason, although feasible – protection. What a sorry sight the groom would be if mugged while packing this extremely expensive piece of hardware on his person. Solution: let the best man carry it. That way, if they are ambushed, the groom can still attend the ceremony without having to postpone the wedding due to injury. Besides, it is much easier to replace the witness than it is to replace the groom.

Oddly enough, of all of the responsibilities that the best man must endure, this is often considered the most important. Due to the monetary value associated with this little trinket, people tend to become a little anxious and irate when we confess our inability to take care of an inanimate object for a couple of days, losing the symbol of their eternal lives together. This has never been excused in the past as an honest mistake, especially at a time when your friends are under so much stress. Adding to all of this is that the loss is never brought up prior to the marital proceedings, but rather, right in the middle of them.

What happens if you lose the ring? Good question. How close are you to the bride and groom? Obviously the answer to that question is "very." You see, the less acquainted you are with the bride and groom, the better your chances for a quick thrashing, then life as usual. But the closer you are to the happy couple, two things can happen. One: they never speak to you again and you lose a dear friend, not to mention that you are as embarrassed as hell. Or two: they forgive you and you feel guilty for the rest of your life because of their great understanding. This guilt will show its ugly face at every occasion too. Sometimes you will be reminded, accidentally of course, of the incident by one of the two. Other times you will remind yourself, perhaps because it has been several hours since your last guilt trip, and you are starting to go into guilt withdrawal.

You never know when an episode is going to come on either. You could be doing almost anything, and the subject will be dropped in your lap. Playing golf, you may have just sliced your ball into the woods, and you might say something along the lines of "I hope I didn't lose it," which leaves you open for many a sharp retort.

Every time you are with a group of friends and somebody mentions the word ring, the couple both knowingly stare at you for a moment, then at each other, as if to exchange information of sorts.

Soon the word ring comes to represent hell for you. It is like watching that Groucho Marx show over and over again,

"Say the magic word and win a hundred dollars." The only difference is that the magic word is always ring, and instead of a hundred dollars, you get dunked into the pit of guilt.

If this really does happen, the losing, not the dunking, you will be able to try what many an accomplished actor, even the bad ones, have done on the screen: lie! You can try to make a big production out of it, and try to con your way out of things. You can pretend to have been robbed, having your house broken into, etc. You can feign illness and try not to show up at the wedding, and claim that you are too weak to remember where the ring is when you are questioned about it. You can even go so far as to emulate those quick thinkers who offer a compromise for the lost ring at the last moment to save the wedding.

Since no ring has been provided, thanks to you, there can be several replacement opportunities. The easiest choice is to borrow somebody else's ring, although this can be looked on with unfavorable eyes, depending on the donor. Usually the person willing to offer such a trinket is either the family spinster, or somebody who has been married many times or recently divorced and they feel that their ring has no symbolism left in it.

Other choices offer even smaller satisfaction, the cigar band for instance, in recent decline because of the non-smoking turnaround of ideals. You can also try to use an earring, although, again, finding the right size can be murder. The well-sucked lifesaver can be a possibility – no, I didn't think so either. It had as much chance as any other food type, for example the onion ring (at least it's really a ring). None of these choices will actually work, although they have been tried in the movies or on television. Nobody really wants to be married with tape or car parts on their fingers.

The ring is supposed to symbolize the eternalness of their lives together. The ring, never ending, represents what their marriage is supposed to be like. It is placed on the finger that has a vein running from it directly to the heart. So if the ring is to be an eternal symbol, let us hope that they can wait long enough for you scrounge up enough cash to replace it. You can only hope that this will be an accepted compromise, but really, it's one of those things that screws up the wedding, leading all eyes and fingers to point in your direction when it comes time to hand out the blame. In fact, the only thing eternal that this particular ring will grow to represent will be your guilt. You will be reminded about it again and again in your mind. It gets so bad that even the ring in your bathtub sends you spinning into a fit of depression. Your only hope at this point is that they get divorced, then remarry each other. Then maybe, only maybe, you may get a chance to redeem yourself. If they decide to stay divorced, it will all be blamed on you because you set the stage for their marriage by losing the ring and plaguing the relationship with bad luck. Don't even try to bring in the adulterous affairs they were having, it is still your fault.

How do you avoid such a catastrophe? For starters, don't lose the ring. I know it sounds simple enough, and there are many of you out there who will remember this advice. Still more of you will follow this advice, but I know that there are still some of you who will follow it to the letter, and still manage somehow to lose the ring.

Sometimes you'd think that the ring has a mind of its own, and it just walks off. Or those darn ring gnomes come into your house in the middle of the night and hide it on you, leaving you to search everywhere. These gnomes are very ruthless and much more dangerous than their counterparts, the car key gnomes. At least with the car key gnomes you can hop into a cab or take a bus, or at the very worst, replace the keys with a new set. They are only perhaps jeopardizing an appointment or a job. But those darn wedding ring gnomes risk a great deal of money and long lasting friendship.

How not to lose the ring – The crash course in wedding management

These are several tried and true tips to insure that the ring will not be lost come wedding day. Of course results may vary, but I'm sure that you will have no problem in using at least one of these methods.

1. Insist that the groom hold on to the ring until you are at the church and the bride is about to walk down the aisle.

Then and only then is he to pass the ring to you. This is a very
solid plan for many reasons. The most significant being that
he who paid for the ring (usually two months' salary) will be
very hard pressed to lose the thing; but if he does, you are
clear of all responsibility. Another great reason is that
churches (and wedding ceremonies in general) very rarely
have open pits, or sewer grates in which to drop the ring once
it is handed to you by the groom. And I certainly don't know
of anybody who can make a ring disappear in the span of
two minutes from his open palm (except maybe David
Copperfield).

The groom of course will try to convince you that you are
a very responsible person and he has faith in you to hold the
ring. He will also try to trick you, saying that even if you did
lose it, your friendship will not be in peril. You must at this
point refuse the responsibility. Tell him anything. Tell him
that you have been a best man at another wedding and lost
the ring. Tell him that you were an only child and would
deliberately lose rings just for the attention. Tell him that you
once dated a jeweler and that you still get flashbacks from
the ordeal. Do whatever is necessary to convince him that
you cannot hold his ring.

2. If you are married or have a girlfriend, have her hold the
ring for you until the wedding day. If you have neither, a
sister (yours or anybody else's) will suffice. In fact, any
member of the female gender is quite suitable. Then, as in
step one, have them give you the ring moments before the
ceremony. Gentlemen, women live for this kind of stuff. They
understand the true importance of the ring and will do
nothing to jeopardize another woman's future. Now I'm not
saying that men are ignorant of these sorts of things, but
really we'd tend to think "no big deal" whereas women
would probably flip out. So, let them in on the fun (did I say
fun?), I meant responsibility.

Again, like suggestion one, suggestion two has many advantages. Blame, for instance, can be passed to her in a crisis
situation. It also gives you the opportunity to pass on your
trust to a loved one (seen as a good thing), and they will take
as much care of the ring as if it were their own. This brings
up a few very important notes that I must mention when
following suggestion number two.

Note 1: If you give the ring to your girlfriend to hold, be careful in how you present it to her, or how you ask her to hold it for you. "Honey I need to ask you something very important," pulling out the ring, "will you . . ." I'd say nine times out of ten you'd never get a chance to finish the sentence. She would be thinking that you've finally come to your senses after all of this time.

Note 2: By no means leave the ring unattended, because if she finds it she may assume that it is hers and start to wear it. This can be a difficult situation when you tell her it is not hers.

Note 3: Be careful when letting your wife hold the ring, especially if your friend makes more money than you do. This type of situation has trouble written all over it, because women like to compare things just like us men do, and in this case size definitely matters.

But if you have an understanding, non-competitive wife, or if you have a very comfortable sofa, hand it on over.

Note 4: Giving the ring to your sister can be a great idea providing that certain circumstances are met. For example, she does not share in the same gene pool as you when it comes to holding onto things for others. Another important circumstance that should be met prior to hand-over is that she is not holding a long-standing grudge against you for some petty childhood situations. Otherwise she may pawn the ring just to spite you.

3. Another great alternative to holding the ring is to hire somebody to do it for you. I'm not suggesting that you pay a stranger to hold a ring worth several thousands of dollars, and actually expect him or her to deliver the ring to the ceremony. What I am saying is to employ the services of a jeweler, for example, to store the ring for you. A safety deposit box is another possibility. Just make sure that you extract the ring prior to the ceremony, or else the bank/jeweler might not be open, particularly if the wedding is on a Saturday or a Sunday.

4. One of the biggest reasons for lost wedding rings is the rented tuxedo. Sure, we try the thing on at the tailor's, but we always fail to check the most important area of the garment prior to wearing, the pockets. Many a ring has been

lost because of a hole in the trouser pocket. Actually I have a theory that there is a conspiracy between those shops which rent tuxedos to you and jewelers. My theory is that holes are deliberately put into the pockets of the best man's tuxedo, specifically to boost ring sales. Then the jeweler and tailor split the profits. This is just a theory and it cannot be proven, but I'm just letting them know that I'm watching them.

The ring bearer

If you are a considerably fortunate individual, the bride and groom will entice the services of a professional ring carrier, removing all ring-related responsibilities from you. These ring-professionals play an integral role at the wedding, and they often fulfill their obligations without incident, carrying the ring on a satin pillow in front of all to admire.

In most cases the guests in attendance are often more pleased with these professionals than with the ring itself. These ring professionals, or ring-bearers as they are more affectionately known, can usually be enticed to perform the ring duties for a nominal fee, a candy bar, or perhaps the promise of some cake.

If the bride and groom are well connected, as they sometimes are, these professional ring-bearers can be borrowed from a relation. The age for one of these helpers runs in the four- to eight-year-old range, but there have been instances where a younger or older version has stepped in to fill the position. When you stop to think that a mere child is preferred to handle jeweled merchandise over yourself, you may feel a bit spited or even angry. But deep down, most of us are glad to be rid of the responsibility, and the children are far more innocent looking and warrant escape with ease when the ring gets lost while they are on duty.

Watching these little cherubs in action is certainly a sight to behold. At one wedding I remember attending, the ring-bearer decided to carry the pillow between his knees while walking down the aisle, much to the chagrin of his mother among the guests, who whispered in increasingly louder degrees for his behavior to stiffen.

It is because of such examples that those in charge are prompted to tie the ring to the clasp on the pillow by way of a piece of string. Sometimes this too causes problems, especially when a rambunctious child is used and an overzealous organizer is too prepared and ties the string in knots. You get to know how good the person performing the ceremony is, making idle small talk as the rest of the guests fight to untie the ring. Sometimes this has been known to last 10-15 minutes, and it has been suggested under these circumstances that the couple simply get married with the pillow still attached. (For future reference, a Velcro fastener seems to be the best alternative to date). This next story was sent in by a friend.

The enchanted ring bearer

Sally was the perfect choice for our wedding. She was Rich's niece and as cute as a button. Rich told me that she used to parade around pretending to be an actress, wearing her mother's shoes and jewelry, wanting terribly to be an adult, and all at the age of eight.

Sally loved Rich and beamed from ear to ear when he visited his sister, her mother. She would dress up for him and pretend to be his girlfriend, simply anything to get his attention. When Rich told Sally that he was going to marry me, Sally cried. She felt that when he was married he wouldn't be able to visit her anymore because he would be too busy with a family of his own. This is when Rich asked her to be the ring bearer. He told her that one of the reasons why he was getting married now was so that she could be the ring bearer. "You see" Rich told her, "they have a rule that ring bearers can't be older than eight, and well, if Pam and I wait much longer, we would have to get somebody younger than you." Sally instantly cheered up and told Rich that he had made the right choice.

At the wedding rehearsal Sally was a perfect little lady. She walked down the aisle of the church like Miss America, so poised and proud that I almost started to cry. I myself was having a little trouble trying to stay calm, and I was so emotional because of everything that was going on in my life, I suppose.

The day of our wedding finally arrived and everything was perfect. The sun was shining, the flowers at the church looked and smelled wonderful, and everybody looked great. So why was I still feeling so nervous? I sat in the room at the back of the church and I started to cry. Sally was in the room with me and noticed me crying and came up to me and asked me why I had tears running down my face. I told her I was crying because I was so happy and nervous. Sally put her hand on my shoulder and said, "That's okay, I cry when I'm nervous too. Like that time at school I had to sing on stage in front of the whole school."

"What did you do?"

"I just pretended that I was at home practicing in front of my stuffed animals."

I couldn't help but smile.

"Do you think that will work for me?" I asked.

"I don't see why not."

About this time my father came in, and asked me why I was crying. Sally answered for me, "Because she's so happy." The music started to play and Sally started to walk out, but before she did she turned to me and said, "Everything will turn out okay." And it did. My wedding day was the happiest day of my life. I still can't get the picture out of my head of all of those well dressed fuzzy animals sitting there watching me get married.

Thank you, Sally, for the wonderful advice.

Chapter Seven
The Reception

"Hey, the wedding is over, I didn't lose the ring. What more do you people want from me?" You're absolutely right, this should be the easy part, and for the most part it is. In fact, has it not been quite simple up to this point? Of course it has. If you have made it this far unscathed, you are doing better than most in your position. The reception is, I'm quite certain, why some people bother to attend a wedding in the first place. Did you ever notice that there are a far greater number of people at receptions than were present for the exchange of vows? I think that some people feel that since they were obliged to give a gift, they are therefore entitled to be fed and entertained in return. There is certainly nothing wrong with this philosophy, other than selfishness. In fact, it is often the cornerstone of most weddings. The father springs for all of the festivities so that his daughter can be showered with things she will not have to borrow, or liberate, from her parents anymore, now that she is married. This is a fair trade in most eyes. Of course, some people take this a little too far, and this is where the best man steps in . . . "buffet police."

I am exaggerating. The reception is a sanctuary for the guests to mingle with friends, joined together to bask in the glow of the newlyweds, their bright future ahead of them. Some of these guests even travel many miles to witness this joyous event, crowded together like spectators at a sporting event. The only difference is that at a reception, they can actually approach and converse with those who held their stares and admiration throughout the day.

The primary function of the best man at the reception is to act as a liaison for the bridal party. To enlighten guests with quips about the couple and remind the father of the bride how much money all of this is going to cost him as you try and stealth some leftovers into your car.

The reception is a time for the wedding party to relax, although few of them do, mostly out of shock. However, they are married, and that was the whole purpose. What happens from here on in should be simple enough – some dinner, dancing and music, a few speeches. That's right, you still have to give a speech or two, don't you? Don't fret, if you are already at the reception, you've obviously prepared so far. Just remember what you have learned along the way.

Reception breakdown

The reception holds several possibilities for today's best man, so to make things simple, we will go through them chronologically; but do keep in mind that you may, or may not, be responsible for some of these duties, as the wedding dictates. These are here merely as a guideline so that you will know how to properly apply yourself when the time comes.

1. The Lull: Once the wedding ceremony has ended, there is often a lull in the festivities (depending on the time of day the ceremony has taken place). Many couples like to have a morning or afternoon wedding (sunshine, birds, that sort of thing), but prefer to have a late afternoon, or evening reception (sunset, etc.), hence the lull. Often during this break, the wedding party adjourns to a serene locale to have the wedding photos taken. You, being part of the wedding party, will also be there, and since you have probably had your picture taken before, I will forego any photography tips. The photographer will tell you where and how to pose.

Sometimes the wedding pictures are taken several days prior to, or after the ceremony itself, although mostly after. Besides, who really knows how long a couple will stay together. After all of the bachelor party stories you will have created as their best man, having the pictures taken before the ceremony might be a bad investment. Keep the timing of the pictures in mind when you are renting your tuxedo, so that you can be adequately prepared without making several trips to the tailor shop.

Another reason for the delay is that it gives everybody a chance to freshen up after the ceremony (hey, some people have been crying – mostly due to your great performance, I'm sure – and they need to reapply their faces). In the case of the wedding party, the shock factor is their excuse, and they can use this time to come to their senses, realizing that, in fact, they are really married. Otherwise they will walk around the reception looking like zombies, or like deer in your headlights at night. All of the flash bulbs during the picture taking usually does the trick to snap them out of it.

2. The Receiving Line: Once everybody is ready to head to the reception, a receiving line consisting of the wedding party and their parents will greet all of the guests arriving (hence the term reception). As the best man, you are not required to be part of this receiving line, and your job at this stage is to walk around and mingle, or to help everybody find their seats in the reception hall. This time can also be used to finalize minor details, or check to ensure that everything is running on time.

3. The Dinner Intro: After all/most of the guests have arrived, everybody will make their way to their seats and wait for dinner to be served. Since this can usually take several minutes, depending on the size of the wedding, wedding ground rules, or small speeches are often offered to set the pace for the evening's festivities. Generally, the head table is introduced as they are seated, and if there is an emcee, he/she will take care of all of this; otherwise, it is your job. But this will depend on what has been previously arranged. For the most part the guests are informed about several wedding traditions that entice the newlyweds to kiss. There are numerous ways in which this can be done. Tinkling on glasses, singing a song to them with the word love in it, having to sink a ten foot putt, etc. Or, perhaps cards or telegrams from those not able to attend are read, etc. Take this time to let everybody know what you expect, if anything at all.

This is also a time to reintroduce any activities that have been set up and possibly initially introduced during your rounds when the receiving line was doing their thing. For example, I've been to weddings where they have had bottles of bubble maker on the table for everybody to blow bubbles with. Or every table was equipped with a little wedding book, so that everybody could write poems, stories, etc., in (in lieu of a wedding register). Still another wedding had the tables equipped with those disposable cameras, that everybody was to use to take pictures of themselves (not the wedding party), so that the happy couple would have pictures of everybody there without having to pay big bucks for the professional photographer.

4. Eat: Do you remember when you were a child and at every holiday gathering you had to sit at the children's table to eat? You're all grown up now and you get to sit with the big boys (and girls). In fact, not only do you get to sit with them, you get to be the focus of attention all evening/day long. I hope you don't get embarrassed when people watch you eat. Enjoy the meal, savor every morsel, relish every bite, because as soon as you are done eating, you get to start the evening off with the first toast.

5. After Dinner: Several things can happen after dinner, from the initial toast to the onset of the evening's festivities. It really depends on how things are slated to progress. It is the time offered to everyone to relax and digest their dinner prior to embarking on an evening of Lambada, the forbidden dance. Hey, nobody wants someone to have a stroke in the middle of the reception because they didn't wait long enough after eating before dancing. That would be one of those super bad luck things that end up spoiling a wedding. Hence, we speak.

This may be the time where the party favors are explained, if they have not been mentioned prior to the start of dinner; or this can be the time to read telegrams, or invite anyone up who wishes to say a few words to the bride and groom. Generally speaking, this is the time when the best man offers the first toast of the evening.

6. The First Toast: Unless there is an emcee at the wedding, you will have the opportunity to be the first to speak. If you are the emcee at the reception, you'll find more detailed information on how to conduct the formalities later in this book. You may have already said a few pre-dinner words, but that stuff was trivial, this is the real meat and potatoes. The first toast of the evening belongs to the best man and is

directed to the newlywed couple on behalf of all of the guests at the ceremony (the best man represents all of them). At this moment, everybody rises to their feet, bringing forth their thoughts and feelings towards the happy couple and their families, and raises their cup in thanks for the wonderful blessing of marriage. This is all directed by the best man, whose toast tries to capture this sentiment and expresses itself through his words.

The idea behind this toast is to basically congratulate the couple and their families, and to wish them lifelong happiness. The wording is entirely up to you, but should reflect the above, and should invite everyone in attendance to share in it.

7. Further Words: The first toast being said, the floodgates become open to several other toasts being offered. They vary from wedding to wedding, again dictated by tradition or time. These toasts usually consist of: a father's toast to his daughter. Her toast back to him. A father's toast to his son, and visa versa. Toasts to and from the mothers, toasts to the bride, toasts to the groom, a toast to the best man and groomsmen (yeah), and a toast to the maid of honor and bridesmaids. These last two toasts can be reciprocated, (i.e., the maid of honor toasts the best man, he thanks her in a speech, then he toasts her and the other bridesmaids, and she thanks him in a speech).

As you can plainly see, these speeches can go on all evening, and really, how much time do people need to digest their food? It's not like they were about to go swimming or anything.

The speeches that the best man may be responsible for, in addition to the initial toast to the bride and groom, are a toast to the bridesmaids and perhaps an individual toast to the groom. Again this can vary, but the bridesmaid's toast is a must.

I won't go into too much detail here about it. You can look to the chapter on speeches for more information. Suffice it to say that the contents of the speech reflect all of the hard work that the maid of honor and the other bridesmaids have done in helping with the details of the wedding, and you are thanking them for their efforts. Again, as the best man, you are representing the entire wedding party and the guests in attendance when you recite your words, so make sure that you invite everybody to join you in the toast once it has been made.

The toast to the groom essentially expresses your thanks to him for allowing you to be his best man. You can say as much or as little as you like on the subject, as you are representing yourself in this matter. Do try to keep in mind length, and content as it applies, because nobody wants to hear you rambling on for three hours about something that they know nothing about. It can be humorous or sentimental or both – just try to involve everyone in your words, even though they are directed at your friend the groom.

8. The Festivities: Lo and behold, I think it's finally time to party! Oh, hold on, you're still on duty. The wedding is not over yet, it's just getting started, but that is no reason to fret and worry about the details of things still left undone. Have fun, you've earned it.

Basic responsibilities during the festivities include mingling and dancing (no problem there) as well as ensuring that no harm comes to the bride and groom's car (see wedding police). You may also be expected to act as purser, and dole out some cash, as well as to supervise the reception itself to make sure that it runs smoothly.

Also, at some point in the evening, you are to organize the traditional garter removing ceremony. I have always thought of this as being somewhat redundant. The groom is to remove the garter band from the upper thigh of his bride while all of the single men in the room gather to watch and drool over this spectacle in hopes that they can take home the garter when the groom flings it over his shoulder. Naturally, having dozens of probing eyes staring at my new wife as I undress her is not my idea of fun, but I guess my wedding is the last place to be insecure, and it is for the sake of tradition.

Having been one of these single guys, awaiting the flinging of the garter, I find it strange that I should be fighting for a piece of my best friend's wife's underwear, that stands to symbolize luck in future nuptials for whoever is unlucky enough to catch it. I think that the chance to obtain an article of a woman's underwear, regardless of the setting, is reason enough for most men to line up and wrestle each other. Whether it works or not, I cannot say, although I do have a small box filled with such things.

For the most part, as per tradition, the bride has to wear something old, new, borrowed and blue, and since women are rather fond of a white wedding, the garter has inevitably come to represent the blue part. My little box proves this.

9. Winding Down: Some weddings can be all day/night affairs, and there is always a time when the festivities seem to quiet down. It is at this point that a late snack is offered to the guests, to revitalize spirits and to absorb some of the alcohol from the more lively ones, hoping to sober them up before they leave.

It is also at this time that the bride and groom often leave the wedding to change clothing, or to gather their belongings for the honeymoon (if they are departing right after the reception). Your job can be a number of things. You can:

☞ Act as driver to take them to and from their destination.

☞ Help them with the packing for their honeymoon.

☞ Remain at the wedding to ensure that everything is running smoothly until the newlyweds return.

☞ Mingle and, on behalf of the bride and groom, thank any guests who are leaving.

Again, this will depend on what was set up prior to the start of the reception.

10. Finally, the Finale: Things by this time have probably really wound down. The bride and groom are walking around thanking the guests, or have already departed. At this point, you may have already left with them, depending on what has been organized. Often, the wedding party retires to a chosen spot to relax and continue the celebration, or stays long after everybody else has left. It has certainly been a long day for everyone involved, particularly the bride and groom, and their concerns should have the highest priority.

If you are still at the reception, just make sure that things close without incident. Make sure that everybody gets home safely, and that anything left unattended has been attended to. And hey, give yourself a pat on the back for a job well done.

Receptions to remember

Wedding receptions can be elaborate lengthy affairs, the hall packed to the rafters with festive guests, or it can be a quaint, quiet, social gathering, with a few friends and family. In either case, the meaning of it is the same. It is a celebration of the wedding, a place to give thanks and express how you feel about this happy day. It is a time to enjoy the personal side of the wedding ceremony, to participate in it. It is a time for family, and a time for friends.

The following stories are not detailed accounts of receptions themselves, but rather a look at the people who make receptions special. I was in attendance at both weddings described below.

Wigged out

The reception at this wedding was definitely an interesting one. The best man always liked to show off his humor and this was certainly a large enough venue to get a laugh at his friend's expense, although it took some coaxing. What they had decided to do, unbeknownst to anybody else at the wedding including the bride, was to play dress up. The groom, Randy, was bald, while all of his ushers sported a full, thick head of hair. Upon their entrance into the reception hall, their plan became obvious. All of the ushers, led by the best man, sported the latest in latex scalps, while the groom donned the most outrageous head of hair, which he wore for the rest of the evening, although it did fall off several times while he danced.

The golden child

Sometimes things that happen at the reception can have a direct effect on you. Now I don't mean that you are scarred for life because of something that happened at a wedding reception; but sometimes a wedding reception can be a source of memories for you other than your best friend getting married.

Being the best man at a wedding of one of these close friends of mine, I had embarked on a mission to ensure that I danced with all of the women in attendance, particularly when I spied them sitting unattended.

I danced with women of all ages, from four to 84, and it was extremely enjoyable mixing it up with the different generations. My downfall, however, was imminent when I danced with the youngest of those in attendance, a sweet little four-year-old girl named Melissa. It wasn't long after dinner when one of those songs, made famous at weddings, was played. You know the type, everybody in a circle doing silly animal imitations. Anyhow, my small partner and I simply had to partake in the festivities, and so we did.

When the song ended, the DJ decided to slow things down, giving those tired few a chance to rest. My partner and I continued to twirl on the dance floor, however, unlike her mastery of animal imitations, she was not quite as adept at the waltz. So I had her stand on my feet while we danced.

When the song was over, all of the excitement warranted a rest and the little girl was enchanted with all the attention that I was giving her. I obligingly accepted her invitation to join her and her parents at their table. Once seated, she insisted on sitting on my lap. However, she was unable to truly control all the excitement of the past few songs and the recent dinner, and this excitement trickled in a yellow stream onto my lap and my rented tuxedo. I hastily exited, downplaying the incident as I returned the girl to her mother, and retreated for cover.

I should have been better prepared, I kept telling myself, but how does one prepare for such a circumstance? Simply put, bringing a change of clothing would have solved everything. To escalate matters further, it was just my luck that the reception was all the way across town from my home and travelling to change would have made my duties at the reception impossible to fulfill. So I compromised and did what any quick-thinking individual would do, I borrowed a uniform from one of the waiters attending us. I then pretended to serve at the reception, claiming that this was the only way the father of the bride could afford to pay for the wedding. I certainly got a lot of laughs out of this, and I kept up the charade through the rest of the evening. I even edited my speech to accommodate new material that I managed to add. The funniest moment came while I was drinking and dancing – one of the other servers came over to microphone and kindly asked me to quit slacking off, and that it was against hall policy for the help to consort with the guests.

Looking back, it was one of the most memorable weddings ever, all thanks to a little four-year old girl named Melissa.

Reception themes and ideas

As a best man, you can help create the mood for the entire reception, and it is in your best interest to take advantage of this fact. If you get the party started, so to speak, people will generally follow suit and open up (not that they need much of an excuse). However, if the wedding reception is treated as a slow somber event, the masses will again follow blindly. So, depending on what mood you wish to establish, the reception is the medium in which to do it.

There are several examples of how to get the ball rolling, and keep it in motion, and I will describe some I have seen, and participated in. Keep in mind that the point is to amuse, not hurt, insult or offend anyone.

Some of these examples are, I'm afraid, "groaners," but since weddings are ageless affairs, there are always some that appreciate the effort, and you could always adjust or alter them to your tastes.

They include:

☞ Key Exchange: Prior to making your toasts, arrange for some of the men/women in attendance to walk up to the head table and return a key on your cue. This is an old gag. The best man tells the guests that since the groom is now unavailable, all of the women present who still have a key to his apartment should return it (hence all of the women coming up with a key). This can also be done for the bride. One variation is to have a very young or very old person come up last with their key.

I myself put an even stranger twist on this at one wedding. I had set up the gag as above, except I stated that all men and women who had keys to the bride's or groom's apartment, to please return them now. That way both men and women came up. I then arranged for the oldest couple in attendance, Elsie and Walt (80 and 82 respectively), to saunter up last, after I asked if there was anybody else. They both walked so slowly, and right after they had deposited their keys, they stopped and looked at each other in surprise, saying:

"Elsie, I thought you told me you were going to the bingo?"

"Walt, I thought you told me you were going to the legion to play cards?"

They did a great job, and everybody got a great laugh out of it.

☞ The Ceremonial Passing of the Cellular Phone: When Dave was a best man, during his toast to the groom, he accepted as a gift from Wade, the groom, his cellular phone, just for the joke. Dave added that since Wade was now married, he wouldn't need his supersecret "babe" phone, the one he only used for talking to women. Dave gladly accepted it and hoped that it would bring him the obvious luck that it had brought Wade. Dave had then arranged for someone to phone him during this speech. He answered and humbly apologized that Wade was no longer available, then he excused himself a moment to talk. When he returned to the microphone, he thanked Wade profusely for the great gift, because he had made a date for Saturday night.

The joke got a little stale when the telephone number got passed out, and the phone had to be turned off because it kept ringing.

☞ Picture This: Daryl was always a prankster and as emcee/best man, he filled the reception hall chock full of surprises. During his speech, he pulled out several "secret envelopes" and walked to several tables and passed them out, instructing people to look at the contents and pass the envelopes around. He then informed the rest of the reception guests that they would shortly be viewing naked photos of the bride and groom, captured at an unsuspecting moment.

Naturally, the newlyweds both turned extremely red, abashed at this exposé, and particularly so when some comments about the pictures were made audible.

"Very nice."

"Oh, it's so little."

"Cute buns."

"I'm surprised they even printed these."

Finally Daryl ended the suspense, and showed the newlywed couple a copy of the photos that he was passing around. They were pictures of the couple, taken when they were babies.

☞ The Slide Show: If you haven't got any naked baby pictures of the bride and groom, may I suggest that you put on a slide show instead.

I was the best man for this wedding, and did just that. I

took as many pictures as I could get my hands on (old, new, Xmas, yearbook, ex-lovers, family, etc.) and with a little help from my friend's PC, some imagination, and a few available afternoons, I created a truly inspiring presentation. I basically doctored most of the photos, cutting off heads and placing them on other bodies. There were several before and after shots. I put the groom's head on the body of a muscular male model, the bride's head on a swimsuit model's body. I put a picture of the bride's ex-boyfriend on the body of a snake, his ex-girlfriend on the body of a hippo, that sort of thing. I took historically famous pictures and pasted their images over top, dubbing their relationship the love of a lifetime.

This went on for over 15 minutes and it was one of the few slide shows that people actually seemed to enjoy. In fact, they enjoyed it so much that both families, as well as several others in attendance, wanted copies of the slides.

☞ Put on a Show (skits and routines): Do you like to act? If you do, then this is a great way to entertain the guests at a wedding.

At another wedding of which I was a part, this time as a groomsman, we organized several skits (4 to be exact) to perform, making fun of the newlywed couple. The maid of honor and I did most of the acting, while the rest of the wedding party were the supporting characters, and the best man was the announcer. We got together a few times to rehearse at best, but most of it was ad-libbed, making it all the more funny. We even brought a few costumes for that realistic effect.

Skit one: This skit demonstrated how the couple first met, and of course, everything was greatly exaggerated.

We accidentally bumped into each other on the street and started talking. She asked me why I was wearing a tuxedo and I said it was because I was a spy. I asked her why she was wearing an evening gown and she said she was hooker. I then remarked that it was a wonderful coincidence, because both my mother and grandmother were hookers also. And the story went on from there.

Skit two: A demonstration of the proposal. I must say, I did a pretty good job making the groom sound like a blithering idiot, stammering out the silliest things, while she looked on indifferently. The bride found this particularly amusing, because as it turned out, this is what really happened.

Skit three: This skit demonstrated what the bride and groom thought their lives would be like after getting married. For this we talked with British accents (still wearing my tux and her gown). I don't recall the exact dialogue, but it went something like this.

We stood looking at each other, then embraced cheek to cheek.

"Oh Darling, I'm so very, very happy."

"Me too my dear, and frankly, hasn't life been just grand."

"Oh yes, and now that I'm president of the company and making a million dollars a year, to combine that with the million dollars a year that you make as a model, we'll be able to build that castle on that island that we always wanted."

"Oh yes darling, and then young Junior won't have to worry about his future."

"Yes, he really is an agreeable child."

"Oh very, I remember giving birth to him, I was in labor a scant ten minutes."

"We'd best be going darling, have Bently bring the car around and we'll go to Paris for a spot of tea."

"Oh, I do so love you."

"And I as well."

Skit four: In this skit, we showed what married life would really be like for the newlywed couple. For this we did a costume change, and returned looking like the cast from Roseanne.

I sat in a chair, a pillow stuffed in my shirt, scratching myself, pretending to change channels on the television remote, while my wife was ironing. The rest of the wedding party acted like children playing in the background. We wanted to copy that Monty Python skit with the family with dozens of children living in squalor.

In a staunch, redneck sort of voice, I started.

"Honey, git me a beer."

"Get it yourself, you lazy bum."

"Kids, somebody bring daddy a beer." (no answer)

"Jeez, you'd think with ten kids running around, one of them would git me a beer."

I then walked to the imaginary refrigerator and bent down to look inside; I even made sure that the crack of my backside was exposed.

"We ain't got no beer."

"Well, if you bothered to get a job, you might be able to buy some."

"That's it, it's time for a nudder family meetin, we're gonna have to sell one of the kids so that I can git me some beer."

"Oh, dear, do we have to?"

"Kids, get your butts in here."

The children then file in and line up. I turn to one of them and ask:

"Jeez you're an ugly kid, are you one of ours?"

I walk past the children pretending to pick one to sell, and I grab a girl.

"Honey, how 'bout this one, she's pretty fat, we could probably get a gude price for her?"

"Oh, dear, not that one, I was in labor for 74 hours with that one, I'd hate to give her up."

"You lucky little lady, I could make some nice pork chops out of you, I could."

I think the funniest part of this skit came when I approached Mike, another groomsman, who just happened to be Chinese.

"Honey, we got a kid here who looks like he's Chinese?"

"Ah yes, dear, that's Michael, we had him after we ate at that Chinese restaurant, remember."

"Oh yeah, well he looks like our mailman."

We carried on for a few more minutes, totally ad-libbing everything as we went along. The hard part was trying to keep a straight face through all of it. In the end, we did sell one of our children and bought some beer. Actually when the children found out what we were up to, they all begged to be picked.

Everyone at the wedding laughed hysterically, especially the bride and groom. We tried to capture certain characteristics of their personalities, and certain things that they were known for saying and added these in as well to try and make the skits seem more believable. Each skit lasted 5-10 minutes, with the best man offering an introduction and some jokes between each one, to give us time to set up what we were going to say. All in all, this was by far one of the best weddings I have ever been to.

Fathers and weddings

Of course it wouldn't be much of a wedding without having someone there to pay for the thing, whoever they might be. Usually, although I'm sure that they wish it were somebody else, the father of the bride takes care of the tab, but not always. In the olden days, when a man married a woman, the father of the bride would have to bestow upon this gentleman a dowry of sorts. This practice is still in use today, however, more often than not, the father of the bride merely pays all of the expenses at the wedding in lieu of a dowry.

In today's world of rising prices, this is not always the most sensible road. Many factors play a significant role in determining this. The father's occupation, for example, or the number of daughters a man has, can certainly act as a stressing factor in this. So, due to the tremendous costs of some of today's weddings, the "tab," as it were, is often spread out between both participating families, as often one income is not enough for the elaborate affair that weddings have become.

Naturally, as fathers, they want everything to run as smoothly as possible, and for the most part, they are quite simply suited, staying in the background all day long. Except, of course, for that wonderful walk down the aisle with their sparkling daughters, but that was the wedding, we're talking about the reception here.

The wedding reception can signify many things to the father. Glass in hand, it is a farewell toast to a loving daughter (unless they plan to live at home), or the gain of a son. It is well-earned money put to a good use, or squandered on frivolity. It is a time to reflect on the years that have passed, a flurry of emotions passing before one's eyes, and only the father himself knows how he will deal with it. To these proud, selfless men, we thank you, not only as fellow men for making the wedding that we are a part of a wonderful affair, but also for doing such fine jobs in raising a daughter that loves and cherishes our friend beyond happiness. You, sirs, are the real best men at the wedding, and we just carry the title, and if it's all the same to you, we'd like to share in that toast with you.

I offer in the following pages some examples of fathers in action at the reception, reminding the reader that some fathers hold more grace in their convictions than others. These next two stories were submitted by friends.

A father's toast to his son.

My father was never much of a talker, but when he did have something to say, he generally got right to the point. He was one of those big working men that liked to put in a hard day's work and come home and relax in a quiet house. Mom would make dinner and we would all sit quietly and eat it. Then dad would go into the living room to read the paper. When he did speak, which wasn't often, he would say things like, "children should be seen and not heard." He wasn't a cruel man, just stoically big and quiet.

When I announced that I was going to get married, my mom cried while my dad just nodded his head in a sort of indifference. So it was a great surprise when my mom told me that dad wanted to say a few words at my wedding. She even told me that he was a bit nervous about having to say a few words, but not to mention how uncomfortable he was. I insisted that he didn't have to if he felt uncomfortable, but he made gestures that mom would kill him if he kept himself quiet.

When the time finally came, dad slowly walked up to the microphone, and what he said, I'll never ever forget.

"I've never been a man of many words, and I'm not about to start. So if it's all the same to the rest of you here, I'm just going to stare at my son for a minute and reflect on how proud he has made me all of these years."

He stood there staring at me in silence for almost a full minute like he promised, as everybody watched him. And then he added, blinking.

"I love you son." And looking at my bride Candice for a moment, he continued.

"And now I have a reason to love you even more."

I got up and walked over to my father and wrapped my arms around him.

"I love you too dad," I said, and he turned after a moment and went back to my mother (who was crying like everybody else). Her moistened eyes looked up at him in admiration as she whispered, *"good job."*

My father had never really ever told me that he loved me before, and watching him standing there at my wedding, I know how he feels and he never has to say it again.

Bad news

Sometimes weddings are not only the start of two people's lives together, but also an end to other relationships.

This is not a happy story; in fact, it's rather tragic.

When Mike got married, it was a big step in his life. His parents had been divorced for several years and Mike was afraid that he wouldn't make a good husband, and drive away his wife, Shari. But he reminded himself to learn from his parents' mistakes, rather than to follow them.

The wedding itself was beautiful. I was the best man and I did a great job, even if I do say so myself. I took care of the reception details and put everything into full swing.

Mike was very happy that both of his parents were there and they seemed to be getting along. It really took some convincing on my part to talk them into it. I told them that this was the only chance they would get to see Mike in a tuxedo, all happy and stuff. I then reminded them of his graduation, when he wore shorts and running shoes under his gown. That was the clincher, they were coming. Of course, I had to lie to both of them and tell them that I wasn't sure if the other was going to show.

Mike and Shari had decided to set up an open microphone to let everybody who wanted to say a few words. I said that there was a stipulation and that before saying anything, they had to sing a song *with the word love in it. Some of the songs were quite funny (I've got a lovely bunch of coconuts).*

Partway through the evening Mike's dad, David, came up to the microphone. He started off by saying how proud of Mike he was and how lucky he was to have a beautiful, caring wife like Shari. But as the speech continued, it became anything but flattering.

David had been drinking and was a bit loud as an individual to start, so now the microphone only escalated things. He started to tell Mike to watch out for his wife, making comparisons to Mike's mother, his ex-wife. He even asked Shari not to be such a b—— over little things, and several other embarrassing things.

It was at this point that Mike stood up and told his father that everybody had had quite enough of his defamatory talk and that he should leave. David just scolded him, insisting that Mike had always taken his mother's side in everything, during all the arguments and fights. He went on decrying his marriage until I had had enough myself and went up to him with determination, but without violence, and grabbed him by the arm and tried to escort him out. He hit me a couple of times, but I was far too angry to care. I threw him out on his ear all the same, reminding him that he had just made the biggest mistake of his life.

The rest of the reception was rather stale for obvious reasons, and many people soon left. With the help of a few non-believers (they cannot believe that it is impossible to have fun at a wedding), we got things back up to a fun level.

I honestly can't tell you how bad I felt for convincing his father to come; I feel responsible even though Mike and Shari insisted he was just being an ass on his own.

It's been almost 9 years since Mike's wedding and Mike has not said word one to his father. He is still happily married to Shari and they both have a great relationship with her father, Bruce.

Chapter Eight
The Emcee

So you fancy yourself the public speaker do you? Now is your chance to impress all of your friends, and their families, as to how well-endowed with the gift of gab you really are. No real need to be nervous here, these are only your peers, it's not like they were strangers you would never have to see again if you really screwed up. These people probably wouldn't be so cruel as to remind you of this episode every time they saw you, and for the rest of your life. Besides, how long can that really be?

Emceeing at a wedding can be as laden with words as you want to make it. The reception, as you have read, can be everything from a simple affair, where people want to relax and enjoy the company of friends and family, to a formal event. People want to spend time in the presence of the couple they have admired all day long. These people are usually pretty easy to entertain. They are not going to turn into an angry mob if you do not adequately entertain them. But it is still important to prepare yourself for the task.

To emcee at a reception is no different than what a celebrity does to host a beauty pageant on television, or a comedian at the Academy Awards presentations. Of course, you probably won't have millions of people watching you, your career depending on your performance, unless it is an extremely large family or you are the best man for a Prince. Mind you, it will probably feel like having millions of eyes watching your every move, hanging on your every word, especially if you are unaccustomed to duties of this nature.

Having participated in several public speaking engagements, as well as teaching for several years and performing the exact same task you are about to undertake, I can empathize with your situation. It is really an overwhelming experience, but it doesn't have to be. The key to success is practice.

Listed on the following pages are things that you will need to organize or be aware of if you are going to be the emcee at the wedding. Several of these responsibilities may not be piled onto your tray, but I have listed as many as possible so that you can get a full spectrum of exactly what it is you may be doing. Good luck.

☞ Spend some cash: Pay somebody to be the emcee for you, hiring a professional to do the job, if the bridal couple are willing. There are a lot of things that require your attention, and you may better enjoy yourself leaving these duties to somebody else. If you are adamant that you will perform these duties yourself, there are several excellent resources available at the library or your local bookstore that will go into far greater detail on the subject.

☞ Preparation: This is your most important tool and you should use it on everything that you do. There are several things that need to be done beforehand, and good organization and proper preparation will go a long way in assuring a successful reception.

☞ Reception Parameters: Before you begin, talk with those who are responsible for organizing the wedding so that you know what is expected of you. This is also a good source of insight and information about the guests attending the ceremony, as well as all those involved.

☞ Research: Try to get as much information as possible on all of the important people at the ceremony. You may have to talk about several of these people, and/or introduce them, and/or work closely over the next several days with them, and it helps if you have some personal working knowledge of them.

☞ Organizers: Learn who they are, from those organizing the wedding itself, to those in charge of minor details, like renting and decorating the car. Then discuss all of the details of everybody's schedule so that there are no hidden surprises.

☞ Attend all pre-wedding functions: Make sure that you attend the stag party, bridal shower (or have someone take notes if they refuse to admit you), all organizational meetings and the wedding rehearsal. This way you are sure to know what is going on at all times, as well as becoming familiar with everybody partaking in these events.

☞ Confirm: Make sure that you confirm and reconfirm all reception details, no matter how small, or how many times other people have confirmed them. General things that are often overlooked are at the reception hall. Things like the air conditioning, heating, sound system, location of bathrooms, telephones, emergency exits and lighting should all be checked. Check the menu details, service staff, supplies of tables and chairs, and backups, etc.

☞ Guests: Make sure that you know the number of guests arriving. That way you'll know exactly what is required to feed them, offer drinks, late-night snacks, numbers of tables and chairs and back-ups for everything. Also ensure that there are ample facilities to accommodate everyone, parking, coat room, washrooms, handicapped facilities, etc. This also lets you adequately time things based on the number of people.

☞ Microphone Check: Very important, because you will be using this device throughout the evening. Take a spare, and make sure that there is an ample power supply.

☞ The D.J. (or band): Make sure that everything gets set up, and that you are aware of his contract (how late he/she will stay etc.). Help him to check the equipment, and have a back-up plan in case problems arise.

☞ The Photographer: Let him/her know what is expected, and the organization and timing of key events throughout the evening.

☞ Food: Know the menu, the timing, coffee service, etc. That way you'll know how to time your speeches and the general flow of the evening.

☞ Plan your speeches, and who is going to speak: Know what you are going to say and when you are going to say it. Also know who else will be speaking during the reception, and when they will be speaking so that you can arrange the schedule and introduce them.

☞ Guest Interaction: Meet as many people as possible; that way when you talk, it is a more personal affair. It also helps if you are introducing some of these people later on in the reception.

☞ Telegrams and Out-of-town Guests: Acknowledge them.

☞ The Head Table: Get to know them, you'll be introducing them, and since they are the most important people at the reception, you will want to have established a personal rapport with them.

☞ Timing: Always keep an eye on that clock to ensure that you are running on schedule. Otherwise you may not have time for something important at the end because you were running late.

☞ Appearance: Make sure that you are dressed appropriately, and that your appearance is professional.

☞ Try not to be nervous.

☞ Relax and have fun.

The formal reception

For those of you who have been asked to emcee a formal reception, and who aren't sure of the correct order of things, I'm providing a list below. It's not necessary to include each and every element listed; choose your program based on what's required by the situation. If the reception isn't formal, you can still use this list as a guide to planning your speaking arrangements, in consultation with the bride and groom. Each element/speaker below should be introduced by the emcee.

Before the meal . . .

☞ Head table entrance

☞ Invocation/grace

☞ Welcome (welcome guests, set the mood and other announcements, like party favors, ringing glasses, etc.)

☞ Announce the order of table service (head table always goes first!)

After the meal . . .

Things to check before you start:

☞ give the audience notice that you're about to start, to allow everyone time for a bathroom break;

☞ begin as soon as the main meal is done, tables are cleared off and wine for toasting has been served;

☞ check that all your speakers, and people you plan to introduce, are in the room;

☞ check that the cake is ready for the ceremonial cutting.

The program

☞ Opening comments:
announce program highlights
welcome late arrivals
brief joke or funny anecdote.

☞ Introduce the head table

☞ Introduce yourself as emcee

☞ Read any telegrams from absent well-wishers

☞ Key ceremonies or other humorous events (see the section on Reception Themes and Ideas)

☞ Out-of-town guest introductions

☞ Entertainment (short skits, acts, etc., by talented family or friends, introduced by the emcee)

☞ Toast to the Newlyweds

☞ Reply

☞ Toast to the Bride

☞ Bride's Reply

☞ Toast to the Groom

☞ Groom's Reply

☞ Special Guest Introductions (family, employer, important local officials, godparents, etc.)

☞ Toast to the Maid of Honor and Bridesmaids

☞ Reply by the Maid of Honor

☞ Toast to the Best Man and Groomsmen

☞ Reply by the Best Man

☞ A few "Talk Show Host" moments: ask guests to call out questions for the Head Table to answer.

☞ Address by the Father of the Bride (thanks guests for coming and welcomes groom to family, anecdotes, etc.)

☞ Address by the Father of the Groom (as above)

☞ Optional: Address by Mothers of both Bride and Groom

☞ Open Toast Opportunity

☞ Acknowledgment and Thanks to Key Wedding Organizers and Participants

☞ Ceremonial Cake Cutting

☞ Closing Announcements:

rest of the evening's program

any "business" – bar closing time and bar arrangements, volunteers required for take-down, order of first dances, gift opening arrangements, introduce D.J.

emcee's final advice to Bride and Groom

☞ Finally, thank and acknowledge your audience!

You may find variations on the list provided, depending on your source. There are no hard and fast rules, so consult with the bride and groom and find out how they would like the program to unfold, and if there are any items they want included which aren't on the list.

As you can plainly see, being the emcee at a wedding reception is no simple task, and I am sure that I probably left out several valid points. The only true advice I can offer in a situation like this is that so long as you are organized and prepared, you shouldn't have any problem. Besides, you wouldn't have been asked to perform this duty unless the bride and groom had absolute faith in you. So have some faith in yourself, and put on a hell of a show for them.

Chapter Nine
Toasts and Speeches

Here is the chapter you have all been waiting for, information about toasts and speeches. So how does one effectively deliver a good speech? I'm glad you asked that question.

Content

There are several things that you have to remember when delivering your speech at the wedding – most important, though, is content. The content of your speech should adequately reflect the people at the reception. You are speaking to the bride and groom on behalf of these people, or speaking to these people on behalf of the bride and groom, and you should therefore try to focus your speech towards these guests, or with them in mind.

☞ Make sure that the material is appropriate for all ages at the wedding (jokes, stories, etc.)

☞ Avoid getting into topics or areas that only a very few people can relate to or understand. Or if you have to do this, briefly explain it to them without going into great detail, i.e., you don't want to sacrifice a majority of the guests, excluding them from your speech, for the sake of a few that understand.

☞ Explain why you are standing up there talking, then get into the main part of the speech or toast, then end with the toast itself, or a conclusion.

☞ Try to combine sincerity with light humor; this usually rounds out a good speech.

☞ Quality not quantity. It is going to be a long day / evening, and senseless oration will just get boring.

☞ Speak clearly and loud enough for everybody to hear you.

☞ Use rhythm in your presentation so that your voice carries meaning, rather than that droning monotone that people all hate to listen to.

☞ Try to make eye contact with people in the room. This invites them into your speech, and for the most part, they will listen more attentively.

☞ Be prepared. Know ahead of time what you are going to say, and even practice it a few times so that you know the direction it will take. Nothing separates a good speaker from a bad one more then preparation and confidence.

If the above list doesn't offer any insight into how to deliver a speech, try at least to keep the following in mind.

The Top Ten things to avoid saying during a speech at a wedding.

10. Avoid making barnyard noises when referring to the bride or any of the bridesmaids.

9. Telling everyone that the maid of honor is really a man.

8. That you slept with the bride in college.

7. That you slept with the groom in college.

6. How cheap the father of the bride is.

5. How the groom could have done much worse.

4. How nice this bride is compared to the groom's previous wives.

3. How surprised everyone looked when the bride showed up to the church wearing white.

2. How surprised you are that the bride and groom managed to stay married through most of the reception.

1. Bragging about how many women at the wedding the groom personally knows.

The best way to get an idea of what to say is to emulate those who have done it all before. That way you'll have a rough guideline from which to work. Go to weddings, listen to speeches and toasts. Watch celebratory dinners on television, for further words of praise, or else hire a speech writer. The following pages offer several examples of speeches performed by people just like you, at weddings across the country.

A toast to the newlyweds

Getting the opportunity to be the first person at the wedding to toast the newlyweds is a very honorable thing. Under the circumstances, however, knowing that you probably couldn't give a speech to save your life, you would be more than happy to pass this honor on to somebody else. Too bad – the newlyweds want you and you they're going to get. The following three stories were sent in by friends.

Satisfaction guaranteed

Joseph really liked to get to the point. He never liked to beat around the bush, so when he suggested that he would make the perfect best man for my wedding, how was I to say no? Joseph was what you might call a lady-killer. He was always dating one or more beautiful women. I would often ask him what his secret was and he said that if he ever told me he would have to kill me. Besides, he would always add, if he told me, that would mean fewer women for him.

I still hung around with him despite his untrusting nature. Besides, being with Joseph was like playing hockey on the same line as Wayne Gretzky; you don't have to be a great player, just rush the net and sometimes the puck will go in off your leg. Many a date I did have because Joseph was skating too fast, and I was there to pick up the rebound.

Finally it happened, I had met the girl of my dreams and things were looking great. Amy and I had been dating for almost two years (this included living together) when I finally popped the question. Joseph was devastated. He wouldn't have anyone to play hockey with anymore, or someone to take all of his penalties and get thrown in the penalty box for being off-side all the time.

Joseph would often confide in me, asking if I missed some of the good times we had now that I hung up my skates. And I must admit he did tempt me a few times, but I was happy. He even said he envied me, and then when I reminded him about it, he denied it.

The day of my wedding was a wonderful day and Joseph was true to his word and made an excellent best man. Although when I praised him, he suggested that he should get paid for his services, and this really gave me a good laugh. He said that he had a surprise for me, but of course he would tell me later. This surprise came in the middle of his best man speech.

"Ladies and gentlemen, friends of the bride and groom, and fellow hockey players, welcome. There comes a time in everybody's life when marriage is the only thing that will save you from such a bad life of dating. This is my boy Jimmy, the worst skater since the invention of ice. But Jimmy, that's all behind you now. You'll never have to worry about tripping over your laces and falling flat on your face again. Just be glad Amy doesn't follow hockey.

"You know my friend, we have known each other for many years, and in all those years I have never once told you the secret of my success at hockey. Well, today being your wedding day I figured that now, since this information is useless to you, I might as well tell you. Actually that and the six or seven margaritas I had at the bar is really why. Besides, everybody else here is either married or next in line, I know because I asked. Okay, Jimmy, here's what you've been waiting to hear for all of these years, ready . . . No, I don't think you are. Okay, okay, I'll tell you.

"My secret on how to satisfy a woman every time.

"Caress, praise, pamper, relish, savor, massage, make plans, fix, empathize, serenade, compliment, support, feed, tantalize, bathe, humor, placate, stimulate, jiffylube, stroke, console, purr, hug, coddle, excite, pacify, protect, phone, correspond, anticipate, nuzzle, smooch, toast, minister to, forgive, sacrifice for, ply, accessorize, leave, return, beseech, sublimate, entertain, charm, lug, drag, crawl, show equality for, spackle, oblige, fascinate, attend, implore, bawl, shower, shave, trust, grovel, ignore, defend, coax, clothe, brag about, acquiesce, aromatize, fuse, fizz, rationalize, detoxify, sanctify, help, acknowledge, polish, upgrade, spoil, embrace, accept, butter-up, hear, understand, jitterbug, locomotive, beg, plead, borrow, steal, climb, swim, nurse, resuscitate, repair, patch, crazy-glue, respect, entertain, calm, allay, kill for, die for, dream of, promise, deliver, tease, flirt, commit, enlist, pine, cajole, angelicize, murmur, snuggle, snoozle, snurfle, elevate, enervate, alleviate, spot-weld, serve, rub, rib, salve, bite, taste, nibble, gratify, take her places, scuttle like a crab on the ocean floor of her existence, diddle, doodle, hokey-pokey, hanky-panky, crystal blue persuade, flip, flop, fly, don't care if I die, swing, slip, slide, slather, mollycoddle, squeeze, moisturize, humidify, lather, tingle, slam-dunk, keep on rockin' in the free world, wet, slicked, undulate, gelatinize, brush, tingle, dribble, drip, dry, knead, fluff, fold, blue-coral wax,

ingratiate, indulge, wow, dazzle, amaze, flabbergast, enchant, idolize and worship, and then go back, Jack, and do it again.

"And now Amy, my being a man, and not to be outdone, I have for you, my secret on how to satisfy a man every time.

"Show up naked.

"Good luck you guys."

Love triangle

This was another interesting wedding. Interesting in the fact that Darren, the best man, had dated Michelle for several years in high school and college and they were supposed to get married themselves before things broke them apart. Several years later, Bruce ran into Michelle and they got to talking about the real reason things went bad for her and Darren. As it turns out, they felt that they were suited for different people. Bruce then mentioned that he had had a crush on Michelle since primary school, and well, the rest is history.

When Bruce told Darren that he was dating Michelle, Darren took the news very well. In fact, he said that he always thought that Bruce and Michelle would make a better couple than he and Michelle had. Bruce was elated at his best friend's blessing, and when it came time for the wedding, it was only fitting that Darren be chosen as best man, knowing both the bride and groom on such a personal level. Darren's speech toasting the groom was expected to be an interesting one, and Darren certainly didn't let the crowd down.

"Ladies and Gentlemen, I thank everybody for attending what I'm quite sure you are well aware is an interesting wedding. I'm not sure if all of you are aware, but I am quite sure that most of you know that the lovely bride and I are very old friends. It could have easily been speculated that this exact wedding might have taken place several years ago, with . . . most of the same guests, only that Bruce would be up here toasting Michelle and me. But such wasn't to be the case. What did happen, as you are aware, is something special and exciting, not only for the bride and groom, but also for me. I have the opportunity to be the best man at the wedding of two of my best friends.

"It gives me great joy and pleasure to know that the two of them are very happy, and I had a small part in bringing them together. I know that many of you are thinking that perhaps I may be jealous or spiteful that Michelle left me many years ago, and now here she is marrying my best friend. Well, to these people I say, yes, you are right. I am jealous, but not because I think that she should have married me. I'm jealous that she's going to interfere in all of the plans Bruce and I have made together over the years. Our yearly trips to Vegas, for example, are over.

"Don't look at me like that Bruce, you don't know the power that Michelle has. She knows my habits and me, and she sure as heck isn't going to let you go on a trip with me. You'll be lucky if she lets you walk to the curb with the garbage with me, and you know, I don't blame her.

"When I first met Michelle in high school, Bruce was my best friend even then. Of course, he was still a nerd back then, I hadn't had much time to transform him yet. Anyway, I would often talk with him about Michelle, the problems we were having, what to buy her for her birthday, the things she liked and disliked, those kinds of things. Little did I know that he would one day use all of this information to his benefit. So Michelle, if you think that he is so kind and caring, think again, he just had an inside track on all the information.

"Well, as the years went by Bruce had progressed from the Darren school of cool, and was ready to graduate. He had even started to date Michelle's best friend Julie. That way we could all double date. Soon Bruce fell in love with Julie, it was kind of pathetic actually, but things were going pretty smoothly for everyone. Then College came. None of us wanted all of the fun to end. We were like the four Musketeers. But of course, as it happened Julie ended up going to a different College out of state. This left poor Bruce all alone again, but not for long. College saw Bruce turning out to be a real ladies man. He would sometimes date two or three women at a time. I had created a real monster. Something changed in Bruce. Oh, don't get me wrong, he was still a nerd, in fact he still is. He just hides it very well. Anyhow, college soon came and went. Michelle and I realized that we weren't such a good couple. Rather, Michelle realized it when I was getting jealous of Bruce, who was having all the fun while I was spending all of my time talking about marriage. It's funny now when I think about it. The entire time I wanted out, Bruce wanted in.

"Well, I got out and Bruce tried unsuccessfully, thank God, with a number of girls to settle down. After graduation he was more serious than ever, while I was more into the bachelor way of life. Then Michelle showed up again. This time it was Bruce who caught her eye, and well you all know the story from here. So here I am still single, and here they are finally married, something the two of them had wanted most of their lives.

"As I stand here jealous of their happiness and my relentless pursuit of my own happiness, I can't stop and wonder if I would now be married to Julie if she went to the same college we did . . ."

Musical interlude

Steve was always a very talented, outgoing guy and my wedding wasn't going to be an excuse for him to suppress his talents as my best man. *I didn't quite know what to expect from him. He had always done some outrageous things in the past, so when he asked me to set aside some time for him during the reception in addition to his toast to the bridesmaids, I must admit I was a bit uneasy. Now I wasn't uneasy in the sense of being uncomfortable, but rather paranoid. But he was my best friend, what harm could he do? Well, what he did made that day the most memorable day of my entire life, and not only because it was my wedding day.*

Steve walked over and picked up his guitar from the case. I didn't even know that he had brought it. He approached the microphone and let everybody know what his intentions were.

He started. "Jamie and I have been friends for a long time and I'd like to dedicate this song to him and his lovely bride Sandra."

The song he sang was so amazingly touching that there wasn't a dry eye in the house, including mine.

The tune is still clear in my mind to this day; after 15 years of marriage I can still remember the words. Sometimes I've even been heard humming it around the house, only to be interrupted by a big hug from my wife.

A toast to the groom

Toasting the groom, or as it is more commonly referred to, roasting the groom, is the long awaited opportunity to tell all of his peers and loved ones stories that only his best man might know. Hey, it's his wedding; he won't hold it against you. At very best it will bring out his character to shine before his new bride, sitting there absorbing it all with a non-revengeful grin, showing everyone in attendance that he does indeed have a sense of humor.

You must maintain proper cooking procedures during this roast, minding not to burn the groom, making him unfit for service, while you sear his tender hide. This can usually be done with modest ribbing, or, depending on the situation of the evening's festivities, with moderate embellishment, for the sake of humor at his expense. Then there still remains the gloves-off, knock-down, no-holds-barred attack. However, this should only be carried out with prior approval, as things can sometimes get a bit messy. All of these things can only be accomplished through the wonder of speech.

If this is the only other responsibility required of you at the wedding, it is by far the most enjoyable. You are able to take any insecurity or misgivings about your public speaking abilities, or total lack thereof, and turn the burning stare of the crowd towards the unsuspecting groom with a few well-chosen phrases. I was in attendance at this next wedding; the two stories that follow were submitted by friends.

Jeff and Debra's wedding

"It has become somewhat of a tradition for the best man to rise at these occasions and describe a lot of the idiotic and stupid things, the embarrassing things, the groom has done over his life. I mean I could say how they purchased a video camera kit, complete with all of the accessories, just so that they could capture every moment of this wonderful two/three day event, and then promptly arrived at the rehearsal with no tape. I could mention how Jeff, in his enthusiasm for getting a glass of wine yesterday evening, tried to put a corkscrew through the metal cap of a screw bottle. Or perhaps how he has in his possession a necktie with a knot tied some four years ago by myself, which he still uses. But, I have decided to dispense with this sort of tradition and relate just a few stories that I know about the sensitive, sensible Jeff I have come to know.

"I've known Jeff about eight years now since he came to work with us at the adjusting department at the retail store. I was immediately impressed with his eagerness, and positive attitude. His desire to keep busy and go about his job to please his employers. My, how he has changed. It wasn't long before he became cynical, just wanted to be left alone and do his job, and was always worried about what time it was so he could go home.

"There were lots of days when I would catch him just chit-chatting with someone. Every 20 minutes I would look around and there he was. He would catch my eye and know it immediately and run away. Then I would catch him 20 minutes later talking with somebody else, there was always somebody else.

"A big turning point came for Jeff when he decided to invest in a house. He found a new focus and became, at last, a mature responsible adult. He came to see the value of keeping money in the bank; and even sold the Mustang that he had coveted for so long. He got it out of his system, as he told me. He stopped buying fancy clothes and eating at four star restaurants. And in time he stopped buying his clothes and food altogether. Ah yes, the joys of home ownership. Now a few of you may not know this, but Jeff has kept a photo record of the construction of his home – right from the first stake in the ground to the laying of

the foundation, to the interior completion. I say a few of you, because I do know the frequency with which this intriguing archive is paraded for view. I myself have had the pleasure on three occasions.

"You may have noticed that in none of the photos is anybody actually working. Well, I gather the builders would stop and get together for the shots, and this was in large part responsible for the construction of the entire street being months behind schedule.

"This brings us to a rather serious . . . and sad point in my speech. A dark time for Jeff, which I feel we must discuss here amongst his family and friends. Coinciding with Jeff's purchase of a home was a time when he fell into a deep and dangerous addiction. That's right, addiction, both physically and mentally. The disease from which he suffered was known at the time scientifically as 'The employee resale shop'. Those of you who aren't familiar with this, it was an outlet for the retail store where employees could purchase scratched, dented or refurbished products at huge discounts."

"It began innocently enough, a set of dishes, a table lamp, packages of screws . . . But the more he put into his house, the worse he became. He had to have more light fixtures, small appliances, pots and pans, cutlery, stereo cabinets, hardware, power tools of all shapes and sizes, moon rays, automotive products, T-shirts, sporting goods, lawn mowers, patio furniture, barbecues, ficus trees; and then the worst of all, his chemical addiction. Jeff had to have every household and automotive chemical product he saw, from liquid Drano to glove box deodorant. Jeff was hooked. All day at work we would hear those pathetic words, 'Hey buddy, if you're not going to buy that can, can I have it?' It became dangerous to get in his way.

"When he transferred jobs to another building, motorists had to contend with his aggressive driving as he raced to get up to the front of the line. Each Tuesday afternoon we would hear the squealing of tires and hide in our cars to avoid Jeff flying into the parking lot on two wheels. Thankfully, through electric shock therapy and the subsequent closure of the employee resale shop, he was saved.

"As for his house, after all his blood, sweat and tears, Jeff can proudly take us on a tour, to show us the rooms he saw constructed nail by nail, and the many items he purchased through work (some even at retail). As we walk over the pillow-like soft lawn that Jeff hand cuts with nail clippers, tip toe through the lovingly arranged moonrays, and peer over the back fence, we can admire the 12 lane highway being built in his backyard. Ah yes, the joys of home ownership.

"Now I might be making it seem as though Jeff is obsessed with his house (and of course Debra), but really he is a man with many interests and talents. Jeff was a member of our company slow-pitch softball team. He showed great ability swinging the bat; fielding, however, was

another story. The first year we played, Jeff was in right field and I played in center. On more than one occasion, I would ease up on the ball, leaving it to him in right field, only to glance over and see him back pedalling to the fence. We would watch him standing poised, glove in the air, ready to catch a fly ball that was obviously about to go three feet over his head. He had a mighty throwing windup, but somehow it would take two relay men to get the ball back into the infield.

"I'm not saying Jeff was slow, but he was always in danger of being passed while running the bases. The very next year we voted to make him our catcher, so as to minimize the impact of his apparent limitations.

"We all put names of different cartoon characters on our uniforms, and after watching his performance as catcher, we aptly named him Sleepy. I'm sorry Jeff, but I must say that if you played for another team, you would have been their designated hitter.

"Now every skier has some great wipeout stories. Jeff is the only one that I know who can boast that he snapped his ski boot right in half . . . walking through the parking lot.

"Now Jeff and I talked each other into taking some adult learn to swim courses a few years ago. He almost got us failed during beginner floating and bubble-blowing because he insisted on standing around in the pool for our four-hour lesson doing nothing but talk. Mostly about girls as I remember it.

"I do reluctantly recall Jeff's country music phase. I would often have Jeff shout to me across the warehouse 'hey dude', that's what we called each other, 'come here', and then right there between the boxes and pallets, I'd be given a demonstration of the latest line dancing moves. I understand it still persists, but he has moved on to the Macarena.

"All kidding aside, Jeff's excitement about Debra was obvious right from the start, and I've seen it grow month by month. I'm happy and honored to be asked to be with you to share this day as they move on to a new phase in their lives and their love for each other. But I know that if Jeff puts in the same enthusiasm, and good humor and care into their relationship as he does with everything that I've seen him do, I know that it will be a long and lasting, joyous time for them both."

Revenge

"Danny, what can I say about Danny that hasn't been said by everybody in this room?

"Danny was like a big brother to me the entire time, growing up. I remember that when I got into trouble, there was Danny. For instance,

the time we followed my dog around for half the day, waiting for him to do his business. Then we collected it in a paper bag and took it to old man Henderson's house, lit it on fire on his doorstep, rang the doorbell and ran and hid behind the bushes. When Mr. Henderson came out, well of course he stomped out the fire . . . in his slippers. We laughed like crazy, although something inside me told me that I wouldn't get the last laugh. Sure enough, it was Danny, thinking about my lack of character, who told his parents that it was my idea. But I didn't mind, because Danny was my friend.

"Then there was the time in high school when we pennied Principal Belluz's office door shut, so he couldn't get out. Yet again Danny was there, thinking about my lack of quality home life, saying that I should spend more time with my parents. And spend time I did, every night for three weeks. But I didn't mind because Danny was my friend.

"But my very favorite was when we were driving around one night, and two pretty girls pulled up beside us, so we decided to follow them. Oh yes, it was my idea of course. We followed them through a residential neighborhood, actually very close to my house as a matter of fact . . . with our lights off, so we wouldn't disturb anybody with our headlights, also my idea. Well, we didn't last long because as soon as we had passed my house and turned the corner we were met by two police cars with two more pulling up behind us. Guns were then drawn and we were kindly asked to step out of the car with our hands up. No problem, I thought, just a simple misunderstanding. Well, before I could even muster some sort of response, I heard screaming coming from down the street. There in their bathrobes and slippers were my mother and older sister high stepping down the block, pleading at the top of their lungs that I was their son/brother 'don't shoot'. Well, doesn't this make for a cozy Friday evening? While I tried to talk to my mother, who I thought would offer a worse punishment than the police would, Danny was busy spilling his guts to the men in blue. Needless to say, he thought that maybe some jail time might teach me some discipline, because they seemed to think that I was alone in the car, and offered Danny a ride home, but got sidetracked by my overactive hormones.

"As it turned out, there had been several robberies in the area, and when somebody saw us driving around with no lights on, they thought we were casing houses and called the police. Of course, when we explained that we were merely following girls, which of course was my idea, or so that's how Danny likes to tell the story; and after the incessant pleading from my mother and sister, the police let us go with a stern warning. Once again I spent many a quality evening with my loving family, because Danny insisted that it was my idea, particularly since I was driving. But I didn't mind because Danny is my friend.

"Well Danny, it never bothered me that you did these, and many other things to me. Looking back, you were probably right. I lacked character, discipline, I had an attitude, and now, thanks to you, I'm a better person. And if I learned one thing from all of this, it is that 'Revenge is a dish best served cold'. And Danny, it's payback time, Bon Appetit. Oh and if you're wondering how I could possibly do this to you, especially on your wedding day, I say this to you: "But I really don't mind, because Danny, you're my friend.

"Mr. and Mrs. Steele, I just want to set the record straight. I know that you didn't think very highly of me growing up. You always thought that I was a bad influence on Danny. Well now you know. And my parents, Oh I wish they were here, all those years they wanted to put me into therapy because they thought I was demented.

"Sit tight buddy, this could take a while.

"Mr. Steele, did you ever wonder what really happened to that new graphite fishing rod of yours? You know the one Danny apparently lent me, and I lost? Well, it did get lost . . . Danny was using it to fish for cars off the 6th St. bridge, and well he got pretty lucky, he caught a bus. The number 9, I think. You should have seen Danny; he played that bus like a pro. He actually thought for a while that he was going to bring it in. But alas, he was merely letting out all the line until, well, it was the big one that got away, dragging your new graphite rod behind it for at least 5 blocks in the process.

"The funny thing about this story is when I asked Danny what he was going to tell his father, he said he'd think of something.

"Oh, Mrs. Steele, do you know your dishwasher that suddenly broke that one Saturday afternoon? Danny and I were in the garage working on the car. Danny was having a lot of problems with his carburetor, so we took it out. It was pretty dirty, and Danny didn't want to spend a lot of time fiddling with the oil and sludge, so he thought that he'd just put it through the dishwasher, then let it dry — you know. Once we got to the kitchen, Danny stood there staring at the carburetor sitting there, dripping crud into the dishwasher, and he had to stop, guilt kicked in. All those years of those parental guilt trips finally paid off — Danny felt guilty. Unfortunately, he didn't feel guilt about putting his dirty carburetor in the dishwasher, but he did feel guilty about wasting all that water on such a small load. So he put all of his tools in as well. He thought he'd kill two birds with one stone. Instead he killed one dishwasher. After all, how was he supposed to know he would clog up all of the lines?

"Please don't even get me started on the microwave. I don't know how many times we've blown a fuse because Danny had put anything and everything inside it. Just be glad they didn't have any pets. Or did they?

"Hey buddy, are you squirming enough yet?

"Heather, lovely Heather, the glowing bride, of course you know I have the goods on your new hubby here, but then I wouldn't want to see you get divorced, at least until after the reception is over. Do you know that towel set that you have, the purple ones? Well, did you ever really find out what happened to that one that went missing, especially after the trouble you went through to get them?

"One day when Danny and I went mountain biking, of course we got all muddy because it rained the day before, and the trails were still wet. The bikes looked a mess, so we hosed them off, but with all of that oil and dirt, they just wouldn't come clean. Now you have to believe me when I say that I really tried to convince him, but you know how easy he brushes things off. Of all the towels he came out with to clean the bikes, he picked the purple one. Again I explained that this was not a good idea, but he insisted that he had done this before and cleaning it would not be a problem. Besides, he said, my bike is worth a lot more than this towel.

"Needless to say the towel never made it to clean; in fact, washing it made things worse. I do admit though, for a moment, but just a moment, panic seemed to cross Danny's face, and I remember that same look when we were in the store where you bought the set, and Danny found out that that style had been discontinued. So the towel just disappeared. That reminds me, I have it in the trunk of my car if you want it back. Of course, you would not recognize it, I don't think it's even purple anymore.

"You know this is fun, I can go on like this for hours, but I see that look of panic on Danny's face again, so I had better stop. Besides, I'd hate to see everybody else here in attendance take back his or her wonderful gifts if I continue.

"I've known Danny for almost 20 years, 20 long years. And in that entire time, good and bad, but mostly bad, you've been my very best friend.

"I love you buddy and I couldn't be happier standing here as your best man. I know that life is never very predictable, but one thing I could always count on was Danny. Now Heather has him to count on and I know that he'll love and respect her and treat her like a lady. But Heather, I just want to give you a little bit of advice. If he ever tries to talk you into doing something, and says that it will make you a better person, run and don't look back till the screaming stops.

"Everyone, this is the groom Danny, and he is my best friend. I wish him well, and I know that he and Heather will have a happy life. So raise your glasses high and drink deep to Danny and Heather."

Hiram's high-tech wedding

"I thought that since Mike and I have been business partners for so long, I'd share with him and Sara, along with the rest of the people here this evening, a little advice that will ensure a successful relationship.

"Last year a friend of mine upgraded from Girlfriend 1.0 to Wife 1.0 and found that it was a memory hog, leaving very little system resources available for other applications.

"He is now noticing that Wife 1.0 is also spawning Child Processes, which are further consuming valuable resources. No mention of this particular phenomenon is included in the product brochure or the documentation, though other users have informed him that this is to be expected due to the nature of the application. Not only that, Wife 1.0 installs itself such that it is always launched at system initialization, where it can monitor all other system activity. He's finding that some applications, such as Poker-Night 7.3, Beer-Bash 2.5 and Pub-Night 7.0, are no longer able to run in the system at all, crashing the system when selected (even though they always worked fine before).

"During installation, Wife 1.0 provides no option as to the installation of undesired Plug-ins such as Mother-In-Law 55.8 and Brother-In-Law Beta release. Also, system performance seems to diminish with each passing day.

"Some features he'd like to see in the upcoming Wife 2.0. A 'Don't remind me again' button. A Minimize button. An install shield feature that allows Wife 2.0 to be installed with the option of uninstall at any time without the loss of cache and other system resources. An option to run a network driver in promiscuous mode, which would allow the systems hardware probe feature to be more useful.

"I myself decided to avoid headaches associated with Wife 1.0 by sticking with Girlfriend 2.0. Even here, however, I have found many problems. Apparently you cannot install Girlfriend 2.0 on top of Girlfriend 1.0. You must totally uninstall Girlfriend 1.0 first. Other users say this is a long-standing bug that I should have known about. Apparently the versions of Girlfriend have conflicts over shared use of the input/output port. You'd think they would have fixed a stupid bug by now. To make matters worse, the uninstall program for Girlfriend 1.0 doesn't work very well, leaving undesirable traces of the application in the system.

"Another thing, all versions of Girlfriend continually pop up little annoying messages about the advantages of upgrading to Wife 1.0.

"There is also a Bug Warning: Wife 1.0 has an undocumented bug. If you try to install Mistress 1.1 before uninstalling Wife 1.0, Wife 1.0 will delete MS-Money files before the uninstall itself. Then Mistress

1.1 will refuse to install, claiming insufficient resources. Sometimes Wife 1.0 self-installs Stud 9.0 into her memory system, giving you accessibility problems to her input ports. This usually ends with a Legal-Doc program depleting all of your resources, suggesting possible copyright infringement.

"There are however, ways to work around this Bug. To avoid this bug, try installing Mistress 1.1 on a different system and never run file transfer applications such as Lap-link 6.0. Also, beware of similar shareware applications that have been known to carry viruses that may affect Wife 1.0.

"Another solution would be to run Mistress 1.1 via a Use-Net provider under an anonymous name. Here again, beware of the viruses that can accidentally be downloaded from the Use-Net.

"Seriously though, I've been friends with Mike for many, many years. And many of these years have been spent working side by side with each other. I know him, I know how he thinks and I also know that he loves Sara more than anything in this world. I wish he loved our business half as much, maybe then we would make some money. Today is the happiest day of his life, because he got to marry his best friend Sara, and I am honored to be standing here to tell you all this.

"I stand here to toast my best friend and his, on his wedding day, and from his partner in business, to Sara, his partner in life, I wish you both all of the happiness and prosperity that a lifelong relationship allows."

A toast to the bridesmaids

Another general responsibility of the best man at the reception is to offer a Toast to the Bridesmaids. This can be, and often is, the only speech that a best man gives at the wedding. It is sometimes preferred to have somebody not in the wedding party to emcee the wedding, and if such is the case, this speech is a requirement.

The speech is basically a way to acknowledge the bridesmaids for all of the hard work they have done to make the wedding a success, and in helping the bride through such a wonderful time. You can usually specifically point out several things that have been done, or offer interesting stories about their lives (if you know them), or how they know the bride or groom. You can also relate how intoxicated they got at the rehearsal dinner when they got up on the table to dance with you.

Crash and burn

Who says length is so important anyhow? I'm referring to speeches in this case, specifically toasting the bridesmaids. They need not be such lengthy affairs; sometimes short and sweet is the best way to go.

Kevin's speech lasted about 20 seconds, 10 if you take out all of the stutters. Granted he was only 19 years old at the time and didn't have a clue what he was doing. All he was told was that he was to be the best man. No worries, he thought, how hard could this be? The wedding progressed with ease. His responsibilities were few, stand next to the groom in the church and make sure he doesn't freak out before the wedding. The wedding had a ring bearer, so no holding of jewelry was involved. Watch them kiss and then go and eat.

It was an afternoon wedding, so there wasn't an elaborate dinner. A light buffet and an open bar seemed to serve everybody's tastes quite well. They had set up an open microphone system for anybody who wished to share their blessings with the happy couple, and a number of people were more than happy to oblige. It was to all of this kindness that Kevin owed his oral presentation.

At the reception, during all of this mushy exchange, Kevin was informed that he should say a few words to thank the bridesmaids for all of their hard work (and because they had to buy dresses specifically for the occasion, where the men only had to rent their tuxes). This all sounded simple enough. As the day wore on, panic started to set in. Was he to thank them by name or as a group? Should he mention the ugly dresses that they had to buy? Should he say something personal? He didn't really know them, so should he find out something and then say it? What if what he found out was too personal and embarrassed them? His mind was reeling, and he became very worried. He asked the groom every time he seemed free, what he should say. He even went so far as to ask a number of other people what he should say, and the commonality was that nobody seemed to know, but a few nice words shouldn't hurt.

The time finally came for him to present his words as a gesture to the bridesmaids. Kevin was extremely nervous. This, combined with the freeness with which alcohol flowed at the wedding, most of which couldn't be resisted, brought things to the very speech I will now relate. There is a saying when you travel, that upon approaching a very small town, that you had better not blink or else you might miss it. Well, the same holds true in this case. If you should blink while reading this next passage, you might indeed read right past it and wonder why the text seems out of place.

Kevin approached the microphone nervously, took a deep breath and exhaled these words. "Ladies and gentlemen, I want to thank the bridesmaids for all they've done for Gail and Bruce. Cheers." Kevin's eyes barely scanned the room to see where the ladies to whom he was addressing this accolade were standing, or if they were still present. His heart was beating quickly, and his mouth was extremely dry. Upon completing his service, he quickly removed himself from the center of attention, or so he thought, and made his way back to the bar for a deserving beverage. A moment later Bruce, the groom, approached him and asked him when he was going to make his toast to the bridesmaids, as the day was wearing on. In astonishment, Kevin replied that he had already given it, and a fine one at that. Kevin insisted that Bruce must have been absent when he was center stage delivering his state of the union address. This is when it was explained to Kevin that he must have made the same mistake as others had throughout the day, forgetting to turn on the microphone.

Kevin repeated his speech almost verbatim, except this time he remarked that he felt like an old pro.

This last embarrassing report was submitted by a friend (you didn't think it was me, did you?)

The Ten shortest toasts of all time.

10. Thanks for coming.
9. Nice Dress
8. Swell job ladies.
7. Good luck.
6. All Right!
5. Way-to-go.
4. Nice spread, pops.
3. (No words-just thumbs up)
2. Cheers!
1. It sure beats cookin, don't it?

I hope that this chapter has given you some personal insight into the finer workings that make up a wedding toast. As you may have noticed, they can greatly differ, and are as unique as the people who offer them. This should be the case for you as well. Only you truly know the bride and groom well enough to say some words about them, or anybody else at the wedding for that matter. Simply be prepared, I cannot stress that enough. Prepare what you are going to say, and say it, and I'm sure when it all has been said and done, you'll look back and realize that you did a wonderful thing. Of course, that failing, there is still always the next chapter.

Chapter Ten
The Generic Speech

The idea behind this chapter is to offer assistance to those who may be having trouble crafting a speech of their own. I simply cannot stress enough that a few well-selected, sincere words from the heart are far more appreciated than a speech that has been taken out of a book. But for all parties concerned, the following is to aid you in developing your own speech from the templates provided.

A toast to the couple

You can start off by addressing the guests, or by addressing the newlyweds.

☞ Generally, an introduction to the couple is the starting point, indicating why you are speaking.

☞ A story or humorous anecdote (some personal words of praise, or a joke) usually follows this introduction.

☞ The toast, or a concluding sentiment ends the toast/speech.

Example 1

"On behalf of the lovely bride and groom, _____ and _____, and the rest of the wedding party, including myself, I'd like to start off by thanking everybody for being here today." OR

"We are here to today to witness a wonderful beginning, the sharing of two lives between _____ and _____, the bride and groom.

"It is to their happiness and eternal love that I kindly ask everybody seated, to stand and join me in toasting _____ and _____ on this, their wedding day."

(Wait for everybody to stand, then offer the toast)

"To Mr. and Mrs. _____ and _____ _____, may they live a long and happy, prosperous life together, forever in each other's arms."

Example 2

"I'd like to take this opportunity to say some words about the lovely couple _____ and _____.

"I've known _____ and _____ for several years now, and I must say that it came as no surprise to me that I would be standing here today, talking to you at their wedding.

"I remember the first time they met . . ." OR

"I remember when they first started dating . . ." OR

"I remember watching them at the rehearsal party and thinking . . ." OR

"I remember him/her saying . . ." OR

"It reminds me of a story about . . ." OR

"It reminds me of a joke . . ." OR

"It makes you stop and think . . ."

ADD INTRODUCTION INTO CONCLUSION:

"Seriously though . . ." OR

"It certainly isn't surprising that they decided to get married." Etc.

ADD TOAST and/or CONCLUDING SENTIMENT

"_____ and _____, I cannot say how truly honored I am that I am able to say these words to you both today. I know, as well as everyone here today, that the two of you will have a long prosperous life together. You are a beautiful couple, and the world happily awaits you with open arms to begin your new life together.

"Will everybody stand and raise their cups to join me in this toast. To Mr. and Mrs. _____ and _____ _____, congratulations, and good luck."

It is totally up to the person giving the speech as to what it will contain. The words should come from the heart, and be uniquely sincere. I have merely shown a rough guideline from which to build. Feel free to add, change, retract, or paraphrase anything mentioned here in these pages. They are at your disposal.

A toast to the bridesmaids

The basis for this speech is as follows:

☞ Address the person to whom you are speaking, and introduce them to the guests at the reception/wedding.

☞ Thank them on behalf of the bride and groom, for their participation and all of the hard work they have put in. You may additionally comment on how lovely they look, or add a joke or further sentiment at this point.

☞ Since there are usually three to four ladies to address, including the maid of honor, you can collectively thank them or thank them on an individual basis. Keep in mind though, that if you do individually thank them, that you are equally thankful throughout your words, saving the most thanks for the maid of honor last.

☞ Ask everybody to stand/raise their cups/join you in toasting these ladies.

Example 1

"I'd like to offer a toast to the wonderful ladies that I have had the pleasure of sitting with all evening, and have had the opportunity to get to know a lot better over these past few days.

"To the bridesmaids _____, _____, *and* _____ *and the maid of honor* _____.

"On behalf of _____ *and* _____, *the happy couple, and their parents, as well as from myself and the other groomsmen, (their names are optional) and everybody else at the wedding; I would like to thank you all for all of the wonderful care and time that you all put into making this day so wonderful for all of us. We greatly appreciate everything that you have done.*

"Ladies and gentlemen, please join me in toasting the bridesmaids."

You can offer a specific toast to the maid of honor after this speech if you haven't included her in it.

"To the maid of honor _____ *who has spent so much of her time and energy helping to make sure that everything ran so smoothly. I don't know what we would have done without you."*

ADD TOAST OR . . .

ADD SENTIMENT

"May happiness reign on them/her for the good deeds they have done today." OR
A simple thanks will suffice.

A toast to the groom

This speech provides the greatest flexibility as far as material is concerned, because it is an address personally from you to the groom, and so the information contained in this speech can be greatly varied.

It usually flows as follows:

☞ A personal story or history about how the two of you know each other, or stories of your friendship and how it came to be.

☞ A story about the groom and the bride and how they met, how he acted, if he made a fool of himself, etc.

☞ A point about how happy the groom has been since he has met the bride (how happy she makes him, and what it is like to put up with him when he is like this).

☞ How happy you are to be there.

Since this is usually an extremely personal affair, it is difficult to instruct you on what to say about your friend, dictating what words to use and how to use them. Suffice it to say that you probably know the groom better than anyone at the wedding (although there may be exceptions), and the idea behind this toast/speech is that you are trying to show everybody in attendance what the groom is really like, what kind of person he is, what the bride has to look forward to, that sort of thing. That way when you are done speaking, the guests will feel that they have been invited to really get to know the people who got married.

Example 1

"I have known _____ for many, many years. In fact we have been friends since we first met in _____ (primary school, high school, college, prison).

"Since that time we have been inseparable, that is until _____ came into his life. She really changed things, and all for the better.

"As I stand here and look at how happy they are together, I gladly turn over my position to his lovely bride.

"I remember the first time when _____ *and* _____ *first met, I'll never forget the look on his face when he first told me about her.*

"I remember looking at him, and he somehow seemed different, changed. He looked happy, and when I finally met _____ *, I understood why.*

"I thought that they were perfect for each other, and obviously, since they decided to marry each other and spend the rest of their lives together, they thought so too.

"I can't help but mention what a beautiful couple they make, and how happy they are together.

"I am glad, no, I am proud to have been _____ *friend for so long, particularly when he makes such a good decision, like asking* _____ *to marry him.*

" _____ *, you are my best friend, and I couldn't be happier for you. I eternally thank you for letting me be your best man, and I look forward to spending the rest of my life not only as your friend, but now as your and* _____ *'s friend as well.*

"I'd like everybody to join me in giving thanks to this wonderful man and his wonderful bride. Here's hoping that their days are filled with the happiness that only the joys of everlasting love can offer."

Preparation

Hey, not everybody can crank out 10 to 15 minutes of oration. That's why most of us don't make our living as public speakers. In fact only about .5 % of the population can actually write a speech about something and deliver it like a pro, making the other 99.5 % of us extremely disgruntled and wishing that they would do this on another planet. But it is because of these powerful speakers that we are inclined to follow in their footsteps and try to deliver, to the best of our abilities, a sincere address of words.

The key thing to remember is that the audience will appreciate a few well-selected words sincerely spoken, more than 20 minutes of non-sensical drivel blathered out as if you were reciting a campaign speech.

You should also not be intimidated into saying anything that is not uniquely you. Don't try to be something you're not. There is really no need to be like the big motivational speaker, unless you actually want everybody at the reception to leave with a great perspective on life, wanting to lose that 10 pounds of unwanted fat, all for only $29.95.

There are, however, those who really don't have any idea whatsoever of how to prepare and give a speech. Maybe you just don't like to talk in front of a large group of people, and that's okay. Or maybe you want to make a good impression at the wedding because you feel that everybody is counting on you. That's okay too. So where do you get this information that will deliver you from the ranks of the pitiful speaker to that of the speech master? There are several places where you can find materials for your speech. It is assumed that you are "in" with the bride and groom, and thus have some personal knowledge from which to work. But sometimes this isn't always the case. Sometimes, you are, or can be, only mildly associated with the couple and really don't know what to say about them, or how to begin writing it. Another situation is that you have an abundance of things to say (a veritable pool of information, if you will), but you don't have a clue on how to convey these things (your message) to the guests.

First of all, the best way to approach this is to prepare yourself.

1. Get as much information as possible on things to write about, the more the better. Whether it is stories about the groom, the bride or just wedding stories in general, this information is a good start. It is always better to have too much information than to have too little; besides, you can always sift out material that you don't feel is appropriate later.

2. Talk to friends, parents or relatives regarding the happy couple, for ideas on what to say. These people have spent their lives with your friends, and are usually more than glad to help in circumstances like these. A few well-placed stories about the bride/groom when they were children (before) and a few others as to what they are like now (after) is a great way to create a speech.

3. Always keep the content of your speech in mind, lest it be a little too racy for the occasion, or too personal to mention in an open forum such as the reception. You don't want to go into a deeply sexual discussion with a reception hall full of children.

4. In the days before the wedding, take notes on the groom's behavior. What you notice and record here can sometimes be the direct basis of your entire speech. For example, how does he act or what does he say? Is he nervous? Funny things he may do or say, because he is worried or excited. That sort of thing.

Sources of speech material

There are several sources from which to "liberate" ideas for a speech. They are always readily available from a variety of sources, and it takes a keen eye to recognize which ones are speeches waiting to be derived, and there are several books available from which to extract speeches. You can really find them almost anywhere. They can come from poems, stories or even jokes. You can borrow the words of others, or paraphrase them into words of your own. You can recite television jingles, or advertising billboards. You can make them funny or serious, happy or sad, thankful and endearing, warning and caring, trustful and sincere. In fact, you can say anything that you want.

Jokes

What exactly is an appropriate joke to tell at a wedding, or to use in a speech? For the most part, the content of the joke should reflect those in attendance. You don't want to have anything too racy, as children might be present. Also try to pick a joke that embodies the ceremony that you are retelling it in. You are at a wedding, remember, and the joke should revolve around this axis. Other humor that is non-wedding related can be admitted, for example, jokes about the occupation of the bride or groom, or jokes related to favorite activities of the couple, etc.

Here is a good example of a joke used in a speech. It encompasses all of the rules of an allowable joke, ageless, clean, relative and most importantly, funny.

Life after the wedding – FOOD AND HEAVEN

I can picture the two of you when you get older, and I hope I get the chance to do this all over again at your 50th wedding anniversary. Can you just imagine these two after 50 years of marriage, both all old and wrinkly. I can just picture them, an 85-year-old couple, having been married almost 50 years, happy all of their lives and ready to spend an eternity together in heaven. They would have been in good health the last 10 years mainly due to Nicole's interest in health food and exercise.

When they reach the pearly gates, St. Peter took them to their mansion that was decked out with a beautiful kitchen and master bath suite and Jacuzzi.

As they "oohed and aahed," old John asked St. Peter how much all this was going to cost, being the tightwad that he is.

"It's free," Peter replied, "this is Heaven."

Next they went out back to survey the championship golf course that the home backed on to. They would have golfing privileges every day, and each week the course changed to a new one representing the great golf courses on earth.

Old John asked him, "What are the green fees?"

And St. Peter replied, "This is heaven, you play for free."

Next they went to the clubhouse and saw the lavish buffet lunch with the cuisines of the world laid out.

"How much to eat?" asked old John.

"Don't you understand yet? This is heaven, it is free!" St. Peter replied with some exasperation.

"Well, where are the low fat and low cholesterol tables?" old John asked timidly.

St. Peter lectured, "That's the best part . . . you can eat as much as you like of whatever you like and you never get fat and you never get sick. This is Heaven."

With that old John went into a fit of anger, throwing down his hat and stomping on it, and shrieking wildly.

St. Peter and Nicole both tried to calm him down, asking him what was wrong. Old John looked at his wife Nicole and said, "This is all your fault. If it weren't for your blasted bran muffins, I could have been here 10 years ago!"

Luckily, there were no bran muffins available during dinner, but I can bet you anything that the dressing that came with our salads was low fat.

Innocence

A prominent pediatrician, Dr. Larry, had trouble writing his best man speech, or more so, had trouble writing what to say. So he went to the very heart of the matter, literally. He had always heard that you should write what you know, and so he looked to his profession for some answers.

He decided to ask several of his patients, all aged between 4 and 9, what they thought the definition of love was.

He certainly received some interesting responses, and compiled them together for his speech that he was to deliver at his friend's wedding.

Here is a partial account of what he said:

"As you may all know, I am a pediatrician, and I became one for my love of children. Well, I had a bit of trouble writing the speech that I am giving here tonight. It certainly is not reflective of the happy couple, I certainly had a lot of things I could say, but I wanted to say certain things specifically, but I didn't know how to say them. Hence my dilemma.

"Basically I wanted to say several things regarding love and happiness. But what is love? Certainly we all have our own opinions about the subject. It's one of those things that everybody knows what it is but nobody can define it. This, I think, is because love is different for everybody. Sure it is a similar feeling, but it is as different as the person expressing it.

"So, I asked some of my patients if they could help me out. I asked several of them what they thought love was, and through their innocent little minds, this is what they had to say.

❤ *Love is like an ice cream cone, dripping down your hand.*

❤ *Love is my dog Sparky . . . except when he makes a doo doo on the carpet.*

❤ *Love is my mom and dad, and sometimes my brother Billy.*

❤ *Love is warm.*

❤ *Love is big and happy.*

❤ *Love can hurt you.*

❤ *Love makes you strong.*

❤ *Love gets you into trouble.*

- ❤ *Love means that you can get away with things.*
- ❤ *Love makes you feel all warm and toasty inside, like drinking cocoa on a cold day.*
- ❤ *Love is like Xmas, you don't know what you are going to get, but you are happy to get something.*
- ❤ *Love is nature, and the sky and the water.*
- ❤ *Love is all around us, and it is inside our hearts.*
- ❤ *Love is like oatmeal, mushy.*
- ❤ *Love is special.*
- ❤ *Love is funny.*
- ❤ *Love makes you sad.*
- ❤ *Love is lots of hugs and kisses.*
- ❤ *Love is seeing someone you haven't seen for a long time.*
- ❤ *Love is like candy, you can never have enough.*
- ❤ *Love is making babies.*
- ❤ *Love is giving somebody something for no reason at all, and not getting mad that you don't get anything back.*
- ❤ *Love makes you act silly.*
- ❤ *And last but certainly not least, 'Love is something that everybody needs to live.'*

"I'm not sure what love is to May and Steven, but whatever it is, they have found it in each other."

Now that you have read this chapter, I hope that you'll be able to draft up the speech of the century. Failing that, I hope that you can say something nice and feel good about saying it. Your friend will certainly be grateful no matter what it is that you say, because you are his friend, and even the simplest of sentiments goes a long way.

Saying a speech at a wedding doesn't have to be a difficult thing, and I hope that this has been properly indicated in the preceding pages. Many a man has given a speech at a wedding, and I know of none that have failed to say what was in their hearts. They all rose to the occasion that was at hand, and truly were the best men that they could possibly be.

Chapter Eleven
Other Responsibilities

I'm not exactly sure what constitutes an "other responsibility." It is for this very reason that I have tucked this chapter at the end of the book. Basically, I have put all of those things in my research that I couldn't properly categorize and bundled them together here. Whether that makes them "other" or unusual, I cannot say.

In any case I have included some quirky stories that may offer some insight into possible other responsibilities that you may be required to perform. These I am sure you will understand when you read the following passages.

For those sure of their duties, as illustrated in the previous chapters, this may act only as light reading material. I hope that perhaps this will act as a good close to a helpful volume of information, and who knows, maybe there are still some loose ends to be tied up. I attended the wedding in the following story, but the last two were submitted by friends.

The King

My friend Rocky was always one to stand out in a crowd. We grew up together in a small town but never actually met each other until high school. I worked at a local restaurant with my friend Carl who went to school with Rocky. It was through Carl that I met Rocko, as he was affectionately called. I still vividly remember the first time Rocko and I met. I was at work, and this hulking 6'2" Asian guy comes out of nowhere, scowls at the aghast expression on my face and says "hey." I was frozen, half-startled and half-afraid. Then he cracks a huge smile and says "Jeez, lighten up, I was only joking." From that moment on, I knew that we would become the best of friends.

Rocko stood out all right. He was the type of guy that everybody wanted to be friends with, and not only because of his size. Granted, most of the population was afraid of his apparent disposition, but mostly because they didn't know him very well. Once they did get to know the real Rocko, they were amazed how such a big guy could have such a down-to-earth attitude. Now I'm not suggesting that big men are all unfriendly – on the contrary. But it seems that most men of this type come across as being intimidating and unapproachable. But that wasn't Rocko. Oh sure, he has on more than one occasion scared the life out of some unsuspecting soul, our modest town and area not highly known for a large Asian population. Rocko can often take you by surprise, and often does this on purpose. Soon afterwards though, a shared laugh warms people over, much like my encounter with this friendly giant.

Many years passed and Rocko was still, and always will be Rocko. He met a wonderful future Mrs. Rocko (Nikki) and not unlike all of his life, typical of his ways, he wanted his marriage to stand out like he had for so many years – but how? One word came to my mind when asked to ponder this dilemma: Vegas. And so it came to pass that Rocko was to marry his lovely bride Nikki in Las Vegas. A small group of friends, a plan and a 24-hour city filled with the wonders of the human soul awaited us, and it didn't have to wait long. We wanted to just swing down, get them married and let the happy couple get on with their lives, but you know how these things work out. Nikki's parents had a hard time trying to accept their daughter's decision to abandon a church wedding for a glitzier locale, but eventually gave in to her plea for happiness. Besides, dad was off the hook for footing the tab.

We got to Vegas and the plan was to be as outrageous as possible. I had suggested the obvious: "What could be better than a 6'2", 240-pound Asian Elvis getting married?" How cool, how savoir-faire, how . . . tacky, and how perfect. But where do we find . . . ? Never mind, we were in Las Vegas, anything was possible. At first, Nikki was not as keen to the idea as we hoped, but with a little bit of convincing and a sidelong chat that if she really wanted, she could always have the marriage annulled due to sanity reasons, she agreed.

We were all set. One big Elvis, one beautiful bride, a colorful city, but wait . . . they simply couldn't get married in one of those chapels. Nikki brought this to our attention. "Mom and dad would have a cow. I can't pick this little thing over a traditional church. They would have me ex-communicated or something." She was right, our plan was falling apart. But wait . . . your parents would object to your getting married in one of these chapels, what about outside one of these chapels? No objections, we were back in business. I rented the Cadillac the next day, pink of course, and that evening we set out to get ourselves a wedding. We were cruising, top down, veil flying, and I must say it was truly a best man moment driving that big old boat. I was with a man who couldn't sing an Elvis song to save his life, although he resembled the "King" in his later years (all things consid-

ered), with big bushy sideburns, and I couldn't help but reflect on the moment and smile.

We pulled up to the drive-through chapel window, ordered some burgers (just kidding, this is serious) and proceeded to get them married. Rocko and Nikki sat up on the top of the back seat while I sat facing them from the driver's seat with the maid of honor. Others who joined in the festivities sat impatiently behind us honking their horns, pretending that they were in a hurry to be married themselves, shouting that the bride was pregnant, and was about to give birth and they didn't want the baby to be born in sin (Yes, these are my friends). The booth attendant/minister seemed unfazed by this display, as if it were a common occurrence, and joined Rocko and Nikki together in matrimony, never once faltering in his delivery by calling Rocko Elvis. We all honked our appreciation a number of times, and 10 minutes after two in the morning, they were officially husband and wife (or so the documentation says).

That having been accomplished, it was off to the reception. An all-you-can-eat buffet that actually served way better food, and non-stop I might add, than any wedding I've ever been to, was the chosen place for our wedding fare. All for $5.99 a person (we all wanted to save our money for the bride and groom to gamble with).

It couldn't be a wedding without drinks and dancing, so we took in a show, where many thought Rocko was to be the entertainment. Then came the drinking. As the best man I felt it my duty to give everybody a roll of quarters and direct him or her towards the slots, because as you know, drinking is free so long as you're gambling.

We drank, we sang, we even danced there among the slot machines and blackjack tables. We even managed to win $150 in quarters. Now I ask you, can life begin on a better note than this? The only hard part was thinking how to make their honeymoon more outrageous than this. But that's another story altogether.

Bed and breakfast

I was asked to be the best man for the wedding of a friend, Stuart. He and I had known each other off and on for many, many years. We live in a small town in northern Vermont, a sleepy cottage sort of town, but very close to all of the metropolitan centers to keep us in the 90s.

Stuart and Nancy have a lot of friends and both come from fairly large families, Nancy is one of six and Stuart has two older brothers and an older sister. These factors became the difficulty when organizing the wedding guest list. Many of the guests lived out of town and would have to travel to attend the ceremony, and you could never be totally certain of a guest's commitment to travel to a wedding. The only problem with this was trying to arrange accommodations for *everyone. It being summer time, several of the usually slow inns were teeming with tourists and travelers, severely hindering the number of available beds for wedding guests. Naturally, being the best man, I offered my parents' house as a possible haven for weary guests, having to travel great distances just to take part in the festivities. Stuart and Nancy were grateful but insisted that this would only be necessary as a last resort. Confirmations from many of the guests had already started to arrive and so far things seemed to be under control.*

The day of the wedding arrived, and a lot of the guests who said they were going to attend, couldn't. They had problems attending due to travel, and time that they simply couldn't afford to take off. Others, who could not attend originally for these reasons, suddenly found that time was available, and simply showed up hoping not to be a burden. This caused a lot of confusion in the arrangements that had been made. Nancy and Stuart's parents got most of the details sorted out prior to ceremony time, but nobody could be fully certain as guests were still arriving.

The wedding was a beautiful affair. Nancy looked simply beautiful, and Stu and I didn't look half-bad either.

The reception was particularly memorable as well, as I recall, because Nancy and Stu had gone to great lengths to have place cards made up for the guests, and since several were last minute, while others were no-shows, this created confusion. Finally, with the help of the reception staff, we brought out additional tables and everybody had a seat throughout dinner. (Some were just edgy from travelling all day, and not having eaten).

The rest of the evening went off without a hitch, considering all of the earlier mix-ups, and it wasn't until 3 A.M. that I realized that the mix-ups were far from over. Several wedding guests, who I vaguely remembered meeting earlier in the evening, were knocking at my door insisting that they were told they could spend the night. This was not a problem. The problem did escalate by degrees as the night wore on, and the seemingly endless stream of people kept arriving. By morning, I had scarcely had a couple of hours' sleep, and was looking forward to a cup of coffee to get me started. When I walked into the kitchen I was greeted by several faces peering over their own cups of my delicious coffee, and reaching the pot that I always have on self-brew, found that it was empty.

Having to wait in line for the bathroom, and doling out the complete inventory of towels also left me a little moody. I even ran into people that I didn't recall meeting during the night, and chalked it up to fatigue, until they told me that they were let in by other guests currently staying at the John family hotel.

I kept good humor about the whole matter solely because I could scarcely imagine what Stuart and Nancy's families must be going through at present.

My parents even kept a positive outlook, having been away for a few days, and arrived at home to find their front lawn littered with post-wedding guests. My father, always friendly, kindly asked one of the guests on the lawn if they knew the family that lived there. To which the man replied that they were old friends. "Really," replied my father in a semi-happy, semi-confused tone, "because I live here, and I've never seen you before in my life." The man's face turned beet red as he stammered to explain that he thought that my father was also a guest at the wedding, and he had been instructed to come here for lodgings.

The day passed without incident, our guests slowly departed one by one until the house belonged to us again, empty of food but no worse for wear.

Stuart and Nancy profoundly apologized but passed on several warm-hearted thanks from all of the guests that stayed at our house. Several of them said that it was the best bed and breakfast that they had ever been to, and others were hoping that they would get to stay there when Nancy's sister Meagan got married in the fall.

Hookers and beer and a bowl full of bees.

I had never been to a Chinese wedding before, but I figured, how different could this wedding be? This is where my story begins.

I was living in Taiwan and working as a teacher, teaching English to children and adults, but mostly children. Now, Taiwan is an extremely financially-aggressive country at present, so there are several westerners to be found working here in the various large international companies that make their home in the bigger cities on the island. I found myself situated in a small town in the middle of nowhere. It is truly difficult to say how small this town is because there are really no boundaries separating the various townships from one to the next. Oh, I am sure that they exist on paper, but there is nothing significant about crossing them in reality.

Being the only westerner in this town, I often found myself the center of attention, being stared at in wonder, mostly by children. The adults have long since seen their first foreigner, or have adapted a better way to look without the obviousness of staring, something the children, innocent and unknowing, have not mastered yet.

I was working for a school where it was rumored that the boss was "well connected." Apparently, as I was told openly by himself and my co-workers, his "connections," were widespread and plenty. This I cannot say with accuracy, although I had never seen the man put in an hour of work while being under his employ, and judging from my pay, I felt that the school certainly wasn't pulling in wheelbarrows of money. And yet he always seemed to have an extraordinarily large sum of money in his pockets at all times. I know this because he openly displayed it to me on several occasions, being sure to open the contents of the roll so that I could be sure that it wasn't simply a matter of folding the largest bill around a series of smaller ones. It was truly a lot of money. It was as if he were afraid that a shortage was at hand, and by constantly being prepared, he would be the town's savior. He also had no problem whatsoever in spending any of it. I had on several occasions myself aided him in decreasing its size, only to find the stack back up to its previously maintained level. Over time he and I became quite good friends, and we were seen everywhere together. I think it was more a matter of face for him, proudly displaying his property, me, a quiet English boy.

As far as I was concerned it was good business practice to let your boss take you out to pubs and massage parlors and lavishly adorn you with expensive gifts. I certainly didn't want to get fired or offend the man; after all, he had "connections."

He also seemed to have a friendly working acquaintance with most of the police officials in the town, something I chalked up to proximity and remoteness.

The time came during my stay when I was asked to attend a wedding with my friend and his family. At first I had the obvious reservations, not knowing anyone and not being able to properly speak the language, that sort of thing. Then it was put plainly to me that I was specifically invited by the groom to attend, as a guest of my boss. Of course I accepted, unsure of what to expect, but happy all the same for the personal invitation.

Now I had been to several western weddings in the past, so I knew how to behave, but I wasn't totally sure about the normal proceedings of a Chinese one. I had heard that there were often several strict traditions that were followed, so I didn't want to upset these scales that centuries of families have cherished.

Most of these traditions are very old and passed down from generation to generation, so that when the children are at an age to finally marry they are afraid not to strictly follow traditions, else live an unhappy life, void of luck and prosperity until death. Some of these customs involve eating. Children are told that while eating with their chopsticks, where they place their hands on the sticks will determine who they will marry. If they eat with their hands at the tip furthest from the food they will marry someone from a far away place, the tip closest to the food, a neighbor, etc. Also, while eating, if any rice is left in the bowl, they are destined to marry somebody with a bad complexion. Somewhat cruel, but effective motivation for cleaning one's plate.

Now, many a match has been made with far more complex considerations than these. For example, Chinese custom warrants that the man should be older than the woman should, and that they should get married when they are both in an even year of their age (e.g., 26 & 28). This failing, due to their ages being an odd and an even year, they marry when the man is at an even age (not as lucky as two evens, but still okay).

Choosing the wedding day is also a complex calculation passed down over the centuries from scholars to the working class. These calculations are extremely difficult, and since a couple's life depends on them, they are brutally accurate. Several variables are considered in the mix, just so that the perfect (luckiest) day can be chosen in which to wed. The bride and groom's birthdays are taken, day/month/year and time of birth, and factored together with days and times of the lunar calendar. These calculations are then cross-referenced to an old chart of some sorts, and through another series of complex calculations, a day is spewed out. Now, often no ideal day can be selected based on this criteria, thus deeming that it is fate telling the couple that they are not meant to be together, and they sometimes separate to search for a better choice.

If the numbers and the stars allow an appropriate date on which to wed, the couple can either get married in their home or at a restaurant. There are some church weddings, but since those similarly reflect traditions of western weddings, I didn't care to find out too much about them. The home weddings have their own specific customs as well, but the wedding that I was currently attending was a restaurant wedding, so I really don't know that much about the more private affairs.

I was seated with my boss and his family and watched as the bride walked in, looking beautiful, and proceeded with her husband-to-be to an area set aside in the middle of the restaurant. At about this time, an older Chinese woman stood up and proceeded to introduce the couple to everyone in attendance. I didn't understand what she was saying, as she was speaking Chinese, but my boss was kind enough to translate. The introduction was much like a business introduction, rather than a personal one. Where the couple grew up, went to school, their careers. Very little about how they met. This all seemed curious to me, that the bride and groom needed to be pointed out to the guests in attendance, but apparently I was not the only one who didn't know them. In fact, having had my boss tell me something about them prior to arriving, I was probably an old friend compared to most. Many of these weddings are similar to the weddings of old, professional associations if you will, where the guest list includes people you want to associate with for business reasons, or to show face by having them in attendance. It would much be like having the Queen attend your wedding, while you danced to Pavarotti singing up on stage.

The woman doing the introductions, as I later learned, barely knew the bride and groom either, she was a neighbor, and had a successful marriage, and an even more successful business, and was perfect for the job.

After the introductions the bride exited, only to return a short time later wearing another dress, equally as beautiful as the first. The groom joined her and the two of them proceeded from table to table personally introducing themselves to the guests and drinking wine or tea with each of them in a gesture of thanks. Our table was shortly approached and I followed suit with my boss, lifting my glass to salute the bride and groom, who seemed grateful to have me in attendance. Some words were exchanged, at which I looked at my boss for translation, and he nodded approvingly. As it turned out, I had unknowingly assented to say a few words about the bride and groom as a gesture of luck. I was curious how this came to pass, but the smile on my boss' face was answer enough. They had heard about western weddings where a man, the best man, offers a toast to the happy couple, an extreme form of luck and future happiness. Well, what harm could it do? I had been a best man before, and being a teacher, I certainly wasn't afraid to talk in front of large groups of people, so I gave it a shot. Besides, I thought, most of them probably don't speak English very well.

I was briefly introduced as the speaker, stood up and garbled out a toast that I am quite sure was paraphrased from an episode of Saturday Night Live; well, either that or the bible. It was certainly sincere and everyone seemed to enjoy my words, strictly for their sound and not their meaning, I am sure.

The rest of the day seemed to pass much more quickly, as I vaguely remember. I was approached by many of the guests in attendance wanting to drink with me. Gan-bay, as I believe was the term, is much like our expression of bottoms up. I have since learned to hate this word as it represents several days of pain and anguish, but at the time, it was rather enjoyable.

The bride again returned to view wearing her third dress of the day, and as always, stunning. They departed and we should have followed along, but my boss, taking advantage of the fact that his family had left, beckoned me to stay with several of the others to enjoy ourselves.

At this point the boss pulled me aside and told me that the groom was so grateful for my touching speech and kind words that he had instructed my boss to "take care of me," and take care he did. We left shortly after and found ourselves in a Karioke house where we were singing songs and being attended to by a number of very beautiful women. We drank several beer, all in 2-3 ounce shots, repeating that *loathing word with each gulp, and I was presented with a bowl of what I thought were nuts. My boss explained to me that the groom had specified that I should eat these, as he was probably doing the same at this very moment, and that I might need them. So I indulged, and I must say was rather impressed by the taste. I soon learned they were fried bees, a delicacy, very similar to oysters in what they represent, but still darn tasty all the same.*

As the evening progressed, the boss thought it an ample opportunity to expose the "wad" and mentioned again that he was under strict instruction from the groom, and started to talk to the girls in the room in Chinese. One of our hostesses ended up being my escort for the evening, and we soon departed. The details that follow I am sure you can imagine.

Days passed when I finally recovered and was met by the happy newlywed and his bride. He asked me if I had enjoyed myself on his wedding night, and I replied "extremely," but was curious at his great generosity, to which he simply replied (all in broken English), "it's the least I could do for my best man."

The sacrifices one must make so that a couple can be happy are sometimes more pleasant than others, but I'm really looking forward to my next wedding! I can only hope that this tradition can be passed along to my friends the next time they ask me to be a best man at one of their weddings.

Alternative weddings

Another thought was that perhaps this chapter is dedicated to the alternative wedding, and again, I am not exactly sure what constitutes an alternative wedding in this day and age. After all, what gets accepted as the norm by a majority of the population can hardly be considered alternative. Still, I'm sure that by definition, they do exist and for the most part they can be summed up as being different from traditional church weddings.

Alternative weddings, as I have found, are difficult to research, because most of them are extremely individualized affairs, and offering advice or insight into them proves an exercise in futility. As soon as you get to understand one of them, something entirely different comes along.

Basically, an alternative wedding can have and be anything and everything that the bride and groom want. It really depends on their tastes and desires. The places where these weddings are held are often the most alternative thing about them. For example, some of these weddings take place on mountaintops, or at the beach, in airplanes or underwater, and the specifics of each one makes it unique to all others.

Many of these alternative ceremonies probably owe their existence to an episode of 'Ripley's Believe it or not', or from some other show dedicated to showing the strange or unusual. Now I'm not suggesting that a person is strange or unusual if they have this type of wedding, but rather that the shows they're featured in cater to such people.

Perhaps this is how they have gained their notoriety. Whatever the case, they exist and they are growing in appeal as couples strive to make their wedding day outside of the norm.

How do you prepare for one of these weddings? Good question, and I cannot truly say. Every example warrants completely different requirements (for example, an underwater ceremony would warrant renting scuba gear instead of a tuxedo, and offering towels to the guests after the ceremony), and detailing them would be redundant.

For the sake of example, I have included a few notes on what may be considered "alternative," and I greatly apologize to those participating in these ceremonies if I have improperly categorized your wedding.

☞ A Naked Wedding: Dubbed as the "Wedding in the Garden of Eden," a premiere Asian "body artist" was wed in the nude before a crowd of several hundred, many of whom paid to see the ceremony. Not only was there a substantial audience present, most of whom were handed condoms for participating, but two local stations televised the event nationally. The groom was somewhat more modest and wore a leaf over his private parts to avoid being arrested for public indecency. A local politician even commented, upon seeing the ceremony, that the bride looked elegant.

☞ Group Wedding: Some of you may be aware of the wedding proceedings of the Reverend Sun Myung Moon, where couples are matched based on pictures sent to the Reverend. He then sorts through the pictures and makes matches from people all over the world. At the recent marriage ceremony on November 29, 1997, 39.6 million couples were united in this single ceremony. This sure puts a lot of pressure on the best man to make a speech, don't you think?

☞ Guest Control: Another recent wedding featured the children from two of the most prominent families of Hassidic Judaism being joined in marriage. The only unusual thing about this wedding was its 30,000 guests. An exhibition ground had to be booked to accommodate all of the people, and arrangements for dinner were also probably very difficult to organize. To make this affair truly individual, however, mostly due to its significance, Coca-Cola printed up special labels on their bottles to commemorate the ceremony (and most people just get matches printed up).

☞ Look up in the sky, it's a bird, it's a plane, it's a wedding ceremony: This is a wedding catered for those not afraid of heights, or falling at 30 feet per second. Basically, the entire wedding party jumps out of the plane and the ceremony takes place while they are airborne. As soon as the happy couple is finished kissing, they pop the chutes and float to the earth. I see two good things in this wedding – short vows being spoken, and not worrying about anyone wanting to interfere. Of course, several things come to mind. Is there an organist, and does the organ have its own chute? What if the best man drops the ring?

☞ Hot Foot: Still another ceremony had the couple, upon completing their vows, walk on hot coals to affirm their everlasting love for each other. (Wasn't the "I do" good enough?)

Conclusion

Well, you have managed to get through this book, a sure sign that you are serious in your desire to be a good best man.

Now all that is left to do is the wedding, and all of the preparations. At least you have an idea (we hope) of what is expected of you. Besides, what's the big deal, it's not like it's your wedding. But it is important all the same, and chances are that you wouldn't have been asked to fill such a role unless you meant a lot to the bride and groom.

You know what you are supposed to do, and what a best man constitutes, and as you have read, and as the name implies, you are the trusted companion, and a man who wears many hats. Try one on, and go out there and be true to your name.

YOUR NOTES

YOUR NOTES

YOUR NOTES

YOUR NOTES

YOUR NOTES

YOUR NOTES